GÄRTEN GARDENS

«Das Licht ist farblos.»
Wenn, dann in dem Sinne,
wie die Zahlen farblos sind.
Ludwig Wittgenstein

"Light is colorless."
If this be true, then only in the sense
that numbers are colorless.
Ludwig Wittgenstein

Dieter Kienast

Photographien
von Christian Vogt

Photographs
by Christian Vogt

GÄRTEN
GARDENS

Birkhäuser Verlag
Basel · Boston · Berlin

Übersetzung Deutsch/Englisch
Translation German/English:
Bruce Almberg, Katja Steiner, Ehingen

A CIP catalogue record for this book is available
from the Library of Congress, Washington D.C., USA

Deutsche Bibliothek Cataloging-in-Publication Data

Gärten = Gardens / Dieter Kienast.
Photographien von Christian Vogt.
[Übers. dt./engl.: Bruce Almberg ; Katja Steiner].
- Basel ; Boston ; Berlin : Birkhäuser, 1997
    ISBN 3-7643-5609-X (Basel ...)
    ISBN 0-8176-5609-X (Boston)
NE: Kienast, Dieter; Vogt, Christian;
Almberg, Bruce [Übers.]; Gardens

This work is subject to copyright. All rights are reserved,
whether the whole or part of the material is concerned, specifically
the rights of translation, reprinting, re-use of illustrations, recitation, broadcasting, reproduction on microfilms or in other ways, and
storage in data banks. For any kind of use, permission of the
copyright owner must be obtained.

© 1997 Birkhäuser - Verlag für Architektur,
P.O. Box 133, CH-4010 Basel, Switzerland
Printed on acid-free paper produced
from chlorine-free pulp. TCF ∞
Graphic design: Karin Weisener
Printed in Germany
ISBN 3-7643-5609-X
ISBN 0-8176-5609-X

9 8 7 6 5 4 3 2 1

Gärten und Natur 6	Gardens and Nature 6
Satz und Gegensatz 8	Diction and Contradiction 8
Eintritt in den autobiographischen Garten 18	Entering the Autobiographical Garden 18
Der Kleinste 34	The Smallest 34
Vielfalt und Dichte 40	Variety and Density 40
An Stelle des Bauernhofes 54	Instead of the Farm 54
Zürcher Geschichten 64	Zurich Stories 64
Illusion und Wirklichkeit 74	Illusion and Reality 74
Wo ist Arkadien? 82	Where is Arcadia? 82
Aussichten und Einsichten 96	Outlooks and Insights 96
Ohne Kontext oder die Liebe zur Geometrie 104	Without context: The Love of Geometry 104
Nochmals neu 110	New Again 110
Grenzen und Zäune 114	Borders and Fences 114
Lob der Zweideutigkeit 120	In Praise of Ambiguity 120
Der neue Gartenraum 136	The New Garden Space 136
Monsieur Hulot im Garten 142	Monsieur Hulot in the Garden 142
Beinahe im Wald 146	Almost in the Forest 146
Der Außenraum muß ein sinnlicher Ort sein 152	The Outside Space must be a Sensual Place 152
Zwischen Tradition und Innovation 160	Between Tradition and Innovation 160
Mimesis 168	Mimesis 168
Willkür und Kontext 176	Arbitrariness and Context 176
Neue Gärten zum alten Schloß 184	New Gardens for the Old Castle 184
Das Ausstellungsstück 194	The Show Piece 194
Gärten in Realisierung 200	Gardens in Progress 200
Weitere Gartenprojekte 203	Additional Garden Projects 203

Gärten und Natur

«Ich bin darauf aus, das Wahre zu lernen, doch Felder und Bäume wollen mich nichts lehren, wohl aber die Menschen, die in der Stadt wohnen», sagt Sokrates zu Phaidros vor den Toren Athens stehend und zeigt somit die Naturfremdheit des antiken Stadtbewohners. An der Schwelle zum nächsten Jahrtausend hat sich Sokrates' Bemerkung scheinbar zum Gegenteil gewendet. Natur ist Sehnsuchts- und Hoffnungsträger, ist zur Ersatzreligion und zum politischen Programm geworden. In der größtmöglichen Entfremdung von Natur erkennen wir nicht nur deren angedrohten Verlust. Wir ahnen auch, daß ohne die Berücksichtigung ihrer Gesetzmäßigkeit unsere Zukunft ernsthaft gefährdet ist. «Schützt die Natur» empfehlen besorgte Zeitgenossen, Politiker und Umweltverbände. Notwendig erscheint uns jedoch weniger der Schutz als die intensive Auseinandersetzung mit Natur. Denn die Verteidigung letzter Schutzzonen bedeutet gleichzeitig die hemmungslose Plünderung natürlicher Ressourcen außerhalb der Schutzgebiete.

Unsere heutige Natur ist längst nicht mehr das «was aus sich ist und sich selbst erhält». So ist Natur in der umspannenden Zivilisation meist nur noch in ihrem eigenen Ersatz existent. Der Wald ist aufgeforstet und krank, die Felder überdüngt und die Stadt angeblich zubetoniert. Da steht der Garten beinahe schon metaphorisch für Ersatznatur, weil er die Antipoden Natur und Kultur zwangsläufig in sich vereint. Wo besser und direkter können wir den sorgsamen Umgang mit der Welt üben als in ihrem Mikrokosmos, dem Garten?

Dies alles klingt bedeutungsvoll und ist belastet von der ganzen Erdenschwere. So daß wir beinahe vergessen haben, daß der Garten zunächst und vor allem ein Ort der Lustbarkeit, der überbordenden Sinnenfreude ist. Jenseits pädagogischer Vermittlung, ökologischer Bedeutung, feinsinniger Ortsinterpretation und künstlerischer Potenz erleben wir im Garten die kleinen und großen Freuden des Lebens intensiver: Das gesellige Zusammensein, den Duft der Pflanzen, die sengende Sonne, den rauschenden Wind,

Gardens and Nature

"I am striving to learn the truth. The fields and the trees cannot teach me anything; however, the people living in the city can." This is what Socrates says to Phaidros outside the gates of Athens. In doing so, he points to the estrangement of those city inhabitants of antiquity from nature. At the threshold to the next millennium it seems as if Socrates' remark has turned into the reverse. Nature has become the carrier of desires and hopes. It has become a substitute for religion and a political program. In the greatest possible estrangement from nature we recognize not only its threatened loss. We also feel that by failing to give any consideration to its laws our future may be seriously endangered. "Protect nature", therefore, is the slogan of worried contemporaries, politicians and environmental organizations. However, the actual protection of the environment seems to be less important than the intensive preoccupation with environmental concerns because, as it turns out, the defense of protected areas somehow implies and often leads to an uncontrolled exploitation of the natural resources that lie beyond the borders of those areas that are being preserved.

Today's nature no longer "exists in and of itself – contained and maintained within itself". Thus, nature, in an all-embracing civilization, is left to exist only in the form of its own substitute. The forests are reforested and ill, the fields are over-fertilized, and the cities are said to be covered in concrete. Therefore, and almost by force, the garden is almost a metaphor for a pseudo-nature because it unites the antipodes – nature and culture – within itself. Where else can we better and more directly practice a careful relationship with the world than in its microcosm, the garden?

The above sounds highly profound and seems to be carrying the weight of the entire earth. We've almost forgotten that the garden is first and foremost a place of delight and of overwhelming sensual pleasure. In the garden – beyond academic mediation, ecological meaning, subtle

die Kühle der Nacht, das Gepiepse der Vögel, das Geschrei der Kinder und den Geschmack des Weines.

Der Garten der Sinne zählt tausend Facetten. Sie einzufangen und in Buchform wiederzugeben, muß zwangsläufig scheitern. Auf hoher Abstraktion bleibend, verweigern wir deshalb nicht nur die Erfahrbarkeit der Töne, des Duftes, der Sonne, des Schnees, sondern auch diejenige der Farbe. Deren pralle Fülle versteckt sich in den feinen Abstufungen der Grautöne der Photographien. Zusammen mit Text und Plan begleiten sie uns auf dem virtuellen Spaziergang durch die Gärten, die damit aus der Privatheit einen kleinen Schritt in die Öffentlichkeit wagen. Dann hinaustreten und kräftig durchatmen.

Dieter Kienast

interpretation of the place and its artistic potency – we experience the pleasures of life, great and small, much more intensely: the company of friends, the scent of the plants, the bright sun beating down, the leaves rustling in the wind, the biting chill of night, the peeping of the birds, the shouts of children, the taste of wine.

The garden of the senses has a thousand facets. The attempt to catch them all and reproduce them in the form of a book is destined to fail. Therefore, by remaining highly abstract we not only deny the experience of sounds, scents, sun, and snow. We also forsake the incredible richness of color. Its vibrant fullness is hidden in the subtle scale of gray shades of the photographs. Together with text and plan, they accompany us on our virtual stroll through the gardens which dare to take a small step away from privacy into the public realm. Then step outside and take a deep breath.

Dieter Kienast

Satz und Gegensatz
Lesarten von Geschichte und Geschichten

«Am interessantesten und schönsten sind vielleicht die von begabten Romanautoren beschriebenen Gärten in den Büchern. In die wirklichen Gärten begleiten uns unsere Wirklichkeiten, die uns nicht immer erquicken; das Leben in seinen mannigfaltigen Anforderungen steht vor dir, wenn du dich in einem Gartenhäuschen mild vergessen möchtest und, als störte dich etwas, entgleitet deinen Lippen ein ‹Ach›.»

So ironisierte der Dichter Robert Walser das verzwickte Verhältnis von Literatur und Leben, Ideal und Realität in dem Zwischenreich der Sinne und der Imaginationen, mit dem sich eine ganz handfeste und zugleich höchst spirituelle Kunst seit langem schon befaßt: «Nun hat die Gartenkunst gewiß ihre Geschichte, und die andere anmutige Kunst, die Häuserherstellung, nicht minder.»

Die Beziehungen zwischen beiden wechselten bekanntlich im Lauf dieser Geschichte, in der Dichter, Schriftsteller und Philosophen eine maßgebliche Rolle gespielt, sich der Gärten in Sprache und Sache angenommen, Theorien entwickelt und in die Praxis umgesetzt haben. Sie führten schließlich vor rund zweihundertfünfzig Jahren auch die Wende herbei, die den Garten, als poetisches Idealbild der Natur betrachtet, aus der tradierten Verbindung mit der Architektur löste und nicht nur in Gegensatz zur geometrischen Künstlichkeit des «französischen» Gartens brachte, sondern auch zur Alltagswelt mit allen Anzeichen der beginnenden Industrialisierung. Diesem Idealbild widerfuhr dann im Lauf der Zeit in den Köpfen seiner Betrachter, was Diderot schon zu Beginn des neuen Naturkults angesichts eines Landschaftsgemäldes von Hubert Robert bemerkte, der ja auch einige der lebenden Bilder im Park von Ermenonville nach der Rousseau'schen Natur entworfen hatte: «Man denkt nicht an Kunst. Man bewundert, und auf dieser Bewunderung beruht es, daß man den Effekt des Werkes der Natur selbst zuschreibt.»

Für Natur gehalten, obwohl sie sich vor allem der Kunst verdankten, begleiteten Gärten und Parks im «natür-

Diction and Contradiction
Ways of reading history and tales

"The most interesting and beautiful gardens may be the ones described by talented novelists in their books. Our realities accompany us into the real gardens and we are not always refreshed by the experience. Life, with its multifaceted challenges, confronts us when we want, perhaps, to gently forget ourselves in a little garden house. And then, as though something was bothering you, an 'oh' escapes your lips."

Thus, the poet Robert Walser ironically described the intricate relationship of literature and life – the ideal and the reality in the realm between our senses and imagination which a very earthy and, at the same time, highly spiritual form of art has been dealing with for a long time: "Now, the art of gardening certainly has its history. As does the other graceful art – the production of houses."

As we all know, the relationships between the two have changed during the course of this history; poets, writers, and philosophers have played an important role and have taken up the theme of the gardens in their language and medium and have developed theories and realized them in a practical way. Finally, almost two hundred and fifty years ago, they brought about a change which removed the garden – seen as a poetic idealization of nature – from the traditional connection with architecture and they brought about not only an opposition to the geometric artificiality of the "French" garden, but also a rejection of every-day-life and all the signs of the evolving industrialization. This ideal picture then went through the process in the minds of the observers, already noticed by Diderot at the beginning of the new natural cult after looking at a landscape painting by Hubert Robert who had designed some of the living pictures in the Ermenonville park following Rousseau's nature: "One does not think of art; One admires. And this admiration is the basis for crediting nature itself for the effect of the work."

Taken for nature – although they owed their existence, above all, to art – gardens and parks in the "natural style"

lichen Stil» die Expansion der Städte und die moderne Häuserherstellung seither als Kontrastprogramm. Erst mit der «Revision der Moderne» rückten auch die Verkörperungen ihrer Vorstellung von Natur als historische Formen deutlicher ins Blickfeld. Damit trat zugleich deren Ambivalenz zutage. Einerseits zur Kompensation städtischer Mängel oft auf zweckrationale Funktionen reduziert, wird «der Garten als Kritik der Stadt» andererseits heute als Teil, nicht Gegenteil von Urbanität reklamiert. Daß Dieter Kienast diese Bemerkung aus dem Buch «Collage City» gern zitiert, ist auch bezeichnend für sein eigenes Verhältnis zu Stadt und Garten.

Den Garten als Kritik der Stadt zu verstehen, heißt ja zunächst, die Stadt als etwas Kritikwürdiges, also durchaus nicht in Bausch und Bogen Verwerfliches zu betrachten, dem nur maximale Durchgrünung und Verländlichung abhelfen könnte. Die wirkliche Kritik an den städtischen Erscheinungen besteht ja nicht darin, sie zu verurteilen, sondern darin, sie zu unterscheiden, ihre Differenzen erkennbar zu machen.

Aber wie, mit welchen Methoden läßt sich solche Kritik betreiben? «Methode ist Umweg», bemerkte Walter Benjamin über sein Verfahren, durch die Erkundung des Vergangenen die Gegenwart in eine «kritische Lage» zu versetzen; und das gilt wohl für alle künstlerischen Mittel und Wege der Erkenntnis.

Ursprünglich war der Kritiker ein Philologe, der die Kunst, Texte zu deuten, betrieb und darüber hinaus eine Kultur aufgrund von Sprache und Literatur erforschte. Begriff und Ausübung von Kritik sind also untrennbar mit geschriebener Sprache verbunden, seit durch die Erfindung der Schrift überlieferte Texte zum wesentlichen Bestandteil abendländischer Kultur geworden sind. Schrift als zentrales Medium der Erzeugung, Bewahrung und Verbreitung von Kultur tritt indes als Grenzgänger zwischen den Kunstgattungen und wissenschaftlichen Disziplinen in verschiedenen Formen auf. Auch «das Bild wird in dem Augenblick, da es bedeutungsvoll wird, zu einer Schrift; es hat, wie die Schrift, den Charakter eines Diktums», schreibt Roland Barthes. Und verdichten sich nicht auch und gerade im Garten kulturelle Erinnerungen und Vorstellungen zu

went hand in hand with the expansion of cities and modern house production as a contrasting program ever since. Only the "revision of modernism" brought about more clarity regarding the incarnation of the idea of 'nature as historic forms'. At the same time, their ambivalence was brought to light. On the one hand, reduced to a purposefully rational function as a compensation for urban deficiencies, today the "garden as a criticism of the city" is claimed as an integral part of urbanism, not it's opposite, not anti-urban. It speaks for itself that Dieter Kienast likes to quote this remark from the book "Collage City" and shows his own relationship with city and garden.

Understanding the garden as a criticism of the city means, first of all, to perceive the city as something worthy of criticism – not something altogether reprehensible which could only be ameliorated with a maximization of greenery and sub-urbanization. The true criticism of the urban phenomena is not to dismiss them, but to distinguish them, to show their differences. But how and by which method can such criticism be realized? "Method is a detour" was Walter Benjamin's remark on his procedure to bring the present into a "critical position" by researching the past. And this applies to all artistic means of cognition.

Originally, the critic was a philologist pursuing the art of interpreting texts, and beyond that, he was a researcher of a culture that results from language and literature. The understanding and practice of criticism are inseparably linked to the written language since handed-down texts have become an essential component of occidental culture as a result of the invention of writing. Script as a central medium of production, preservation, and the spreading of culture, however, takes on the role of intermediary between the different types of artistic and scientific disciplines. It can even be said that "the picture becomes a script in that moment when it becomes meaningful; it has, like the script, the character of a dictum", writes Roland Barthes. And isn't it true that, especially in the garden, cultural memories and ideas condense into meaningful pictures which, in a remote sense, can be understood as "texts"?

Analogous with the criticism of text in a philological sense, the garden-historian Marie-Luise Gothein noted at

bedeutungsvollen Bildern, die als «Texte» im weitesten Sinne zu verstehen sind?

Analog zur Textkritik im philologischen Sinne bemerkte die Gartenkunsthistorikerin Marie-Luise Gothein zu Beginn des zwanzigsten Jahrhunderts eine Hauptschwierigkeit beim Studium alter Gärten darin, daß «das Vorhandene wie ein verderbter Text immer erst durch Vergleich mit alten Abbildungen und Nachrichten in seinem ursprünglichen Zustande wiederhergestellt werden mußte». Aber auch neue Gärten wurden damals schon mit Geschriebenem verglichen. So sah Hugo von Hofmannsthal beispielsweise manchen seiner Zeitgenossen in der Anlage eines «Gartens seine stumme Biographie schreiben». Mit dem betonten Interesse an Geschichte und Geschichten haben gegen Ende dieses Jahrhunderts die Verweise auf Lesbarkeit auch in den Konzepten neuer Gärten zugenommen. Von Semantik und Grammatik, Syntax und Vokabular ist da die Rede, von entziffern, zitieren und übersetzen.

Michel Foucault, für den der Garten «eine selige und universalisierende Heterotopie» ist, schlägt zu ihrer Erkundung und Darstellung eine «Heterotopologie» vor, deren Aufgabe «das Studium, die Analyse, die Beschreibung, die ‹Lektüre› (wie man jetzt gern sagt) dieser verschiedenen Räume, dieser anderen Orte wäre: gewissermaßen eine zugleich mythische und reale Bestreitung des Raumes, in dem wir leben». Doch während Mythen dazu neigen, Geschichte in Natur zu verwandeln, verfährt die kritische Lektüre von Gärten, dieses besonderen Kapitels menschlicher Geschichte der Natur, eher umgekehrt.

«Gärten können gelesen und der Zeit gemäß interpretiert werden», meint auch Dieter Kienast. Mit aktuellen Bezügen greift er die alte Tradition, das Wirkliche wie einen Text zu lesen, wieder auf. Aber was ist, was war ursprünglich das Motiv für den Gebrauch dieser Metaphorik?

Nach Hans Blumenbergs Ausführungen über die «Lesbarkeit der Welt» ist der Wunsch, «die Welt möge sich in anderer Weise als der der bloßen Wahrnehmung... ihrer Erscheinungen zugänglich erweisen: im Aggregatzustand der ‹Lesbarkeit› als ein Ganzes von Natur, Leben und Geschichte sinnspendend sich erschließen, ... gewiß kein naturwüchsiges Bedürfnis», gehört aber dennoch «zum

the beginning of the twentieth century that one of the main difficulties in the study of old gardens is that "the existing had to be recreated in its original state by comparing it first with old pictures and news reports, like a damaged text." However, even back then, new gardens were already being compared with writings. Hugo von Hofmannsthal, for example, saw some of his contemporaries "write his silent biography" by laying-out a garden. The enhanced interest in history and tales has led to an increase in references to readability at the end of this century of the concepts of new gardens. Semantics and grammar, syntax and vocabulary are being talked about, deciphered, quoted and translated.

Michel Foucault, for whom the garden is "a blessed and universalizing heterotopy", for its discovery and presentation, suggests a "heterotopology" the task of which would be "the study, analysis, description – the 'lecture' (which nowadays seems to be a favorable expression) – of these different spaces, these other places: a mythical and, at the same time, real dispute of the space we live in, so to speak". However, while myths have the tendency to transform history into nature, the critical lecture of gardens, of this special chapter of humankind's history of nature, rather proceeds the other way around.

Dieter Kienast also believes that "gardens can be read and interpreted according to the times". He takes up the old tradition of reading reality like a text with current references. But what is and was the motif for the use of this metaphor originally?

According to Hans Blumenberg's explanations about the "readability of the world", the desire that "the world would prove to be accessible in a way other than by mere observation ... of its phenomena, that it would sensibly disclose itself as a whole, consisting of nature, life and history, in the aggregate condition of 'readability', ... is definitely not a naturally growing need". However, it still belongs to "the essence of the demand that a sense or meaning be derived from reality, directed to its most perfect and no longer forceful availability". Two hundred and fifty years ago, the "English garden", therefore, turned against the "rape of nature", that the Duke of Saint Simon

Inbegriff des Sinnverlangens an die Realität, gerichtet auf ihre vollkommenste und nicht mehr gewaltsame Verfügbarkeit».

Gegen die «Vergewaltigung der Natur», wie sie schon der Herzog von Saint Simon in den Gärten von Versailles sah, hatte sich ja vor rund zweihundertfünfzig Jahren auch der «englische Garten» gewandt.

Statt der tabula rasa, die sich so mancher Idealstadtbauer und Häuserhersteller als Bauplatz wünschte oder gewaltsam schuf, bevorzugten Gartenarchitekten in der Tradition der Moderne, die mit dem «natürlichen Stil» begann, ein mannigfaltiges Terrain und folgten darin den Zeichen des genius loci.

«Aus der Lektüre und Analyse des Ortes» suchen auch Dieter Kienast und seine Mitarbeiter die Grundkonzeption für einen Garten zu gewinnen, die «Beliebigkeit und Austauschbarkeit der Lösungen verhindern» soll. Die zeitgemäße Wendung in der Kunst, die «capabilities», die Möglichkeiten eines Ortes zu nutzen, um seine Unverwechselbarkeit, auf die es Dieter Kienast ankommt, zu erhalten und zu akzentuieren, führt allerdings heute zu anderen Rücksichten und Aufmerksamkeiten als zur Zeit der beginnenden Industrialisierung. Hatte damals «Natur» den Widerpart zur Alltagswelt übernommen, so tritt heute angesichts verschärfter technologisch und ökonomisch bedingter Entfremdungsprozesse bei gleichzeitigem Abbau industrieller Arbeitsplätze – und vielleicht auch mit Blick auf eine immer unsicherer erscheinende Zukunft – «Geschichte» allenthalben als der andere Zeit-Raum auf, an dem sich auch die Umwandlung von Restflächen und Industriebrachen in Gärten und Parks orientiert.

«Geschichte» ist jedoch ein doppelgesichtiges Wort. Es meint zugleich das Geschehen und den Bericht davon; das, was dem Ort, was am Ort geschah, und das, was der Ort, was man vom Ort erzählt. Das eine läßt sich indes vom anderen nicht trennen. Geschichte ist immer auch erzählende, berichtende Sprache.

Die Sprache des Ortes, mit der Garten- und Landschaftsarchitektur in ihrer «Schreibweise» korrespondiert, läßt viele verschiedene Lesarten zu. Wohin führen heute Erinnerung, Spurensicherung und Neu-Interpretation des ge-

had, even at that early date, seen in the gardens at Versailles.

Instead of the tabula rasa desired or violently created by the idealistic city designers and house producers as a building lot, the garden architects preferred a multifaceted terrain following the signs of the genius loci in the tradition of modernism, which started with the "natural style".

Dieter Kienast and his collaborators strive to gain the basic concept for a garden "from the analysis and lecture of the location", which would "prevent an arbitrariness and exchangeability of the solutions." However, the contemporary turn in the art to a use of the capabilities of a location in order to maintain and accentuate its uniqueness, which is what Dieter Kienast is always looking for, leads, today, to other conclusions and attentiveness than those that existed during the time of the onset of industrialization. While, at that time, "nature" had taken on the counterpart of every-day-life, today, "history" enters the scene as the other time-space, toward which the transformation of remnant surfaces and industrial fallow land into gardens and parks is oriented. The reason for this is the ever accelerating process of estrangement as a result of a technological economy and, at the same time, a decreasing industrial economy and, therefore, perhaps the outlook to an ever more insecure future.

"History", however, is a two-sided word. It describes the events and reports what happened to the location, at the location and it describes what the location communicates and what one tells about it. One can not be separated from the other. History is always a telling, reporting language.

The language of the location, to which the garden and landscape architecture corresponds in its "spelling", allows for various ways of reading it. Where does memory, the collection of evidence, and the reinterpretation of the genius loci lead to? To a world of pictures, where past times are illustrated in an illusory way, like nature once depicting nature, or to places where non-simultaneous events confront each other dialectically and stimulate our ability to differentiate? To the imploring idea of history or to history as a continuous process?

nius loci? Zu einer Welt von Bildern, worin vergangene Zeiten illusionistisch veranschaulicht werden wie einst Natur nach der Natur, oder zu Orten, an denen sich Ungleichzeitigkeiten dialektisch reiben und das Unterscheidungsvermögen anregen? Zur beschwörenden Idee von Geschichte oder zur Geschichte als fortwährendem Prozeß?

«Garten- und Landschaftsarchitektur ist Spiegel der Zeit. Es sollen die aktuellen ökonomischen, ökologischen, sozialen und technischen Randbedingungen sichtbar werden», schreibt Dieter Kienast; und das läßt sich angesichts von ihm entworfener Gärten und Parks bisweilen auch ganz wörtlich oder vielmehr räumlich verstehen. Anders als die blickdicht umhegten Ideallandschaften en miniature aus romantischer Vergangenheit beziehen sich diese Gärten und Parks in ihrer Eigenart noch dezidiert auf Angrenzendes, Umgebendes; das vielfältig Heterogene der Stadt wird nicht verdrängt. Das zeigen die Entwürfe für den neuen Günthersburgpark in Frankfurt und den Park am Moabiter Werder in Berlin; es bestätigt sich auch im eigenen, «in dauernder Ausführung» begriffenen Garten an der Thujastraße in Zürich.

«Wenn wir Gartenarchitektur als Auseinandersetzung mit den aktuellen Zeitereignissen verstehen», heißt das für Dieter Kienast, «auch Einbezug des weiteren kulturellen Umfeldes». Gemeint sind damit Bereiche von Kunst und Wissenschaft wie Film und Video, Musik, Literatur und Philosophie, kurzum alles, was mehr als das «arm Zweckmäßige» produziert.

«Ein Teil der Krise rezenter Gartenarchitektur», so meint Dieter Kienast, «beruht wohl auf der Tatsache, daß wir so entsetzlich zweckbestimmt sind und die Sinnfrage der bewährten Obhut der Altphilologie überlassen». Darum sollen Gärten und Parks nicht nur «von ihrer Geschichte erzählen», sondern «auch neue Geschichten erzählen. Sie sind poetische Orte unserer Vergangenheit, Gegenwart und Zukunft». Es geht also um die doppelte Funktion ihrer «Schreibweise»: die kritische und die poetische. Gemeinsamkeit mit der Poesie hat der Garten in der Tat ja nicht nur als Träger literarischer Vorstellungen, sondern auch in der korrespondierenden raum-zeitlichen Organisation. Die Zeit-Struktur der Verschränkung von Vergangenheit, Gegen-

"Garden and landscape architecture is the mirror of time. The current economic, socio-ecological and technical framework conditions should become visible", writes Dieter Kienast. And considering the gardens and parks designed by him, this can be understood literally, or rather, spatially. As opposed to the impenetrably cared-for ideal landscapes en miniature from a romantic past, these gardens and parks refer in their uniqueness to the surroundings, the environment; the abundance of the heterogeneous city is not pushed away. The designs for the Günthersburg park in Frankfurt and the park at the Moabit Werder in Berlin illustrate this and it is being confirmed in his own, "in continuous realization" at Thujastrasse in Zurich.

"If we understand garden architecture as a dispute with the current events of time, it also means", for Dieter Kienast, "the inclusion of the further cultural environment". He means the realms of art and science such as film, video, music, literature and philosophy. In brief: everything producing more than the "poorly purposeful".

"Part of the crisis in recent garden architecture is based on the fact that we are so terribly purposeful and leave the question of reason and sense to the proven care of the old philology", says Kienast. Therefore, gardens and parks should not only "tell about their history", but also "tell new stories. They are poetic places of our past, present and future". The point being the double function of their "spelling": the critical and the poetic one. In fact, the garden does have something in common with poetry not only as a carrier of literary imaginations, but also in the corresponding organization of space and time. The time-structure of the overlapping of past, present and future is, in Novalis' view, characteristic for the art of poetry, about which he writes: "Nothing is more poetic than memory and a sense or idea of the future. The usual present connects past and future by limitation. However, there is a spiritual present which identifies both by dissolution, and this mixture is the element, the atmosphere of the poet."

The unusual present of poetry, therefore, is not a point on an eternal time-line reaching from past to future, but stretches out as an esthetic time-frame with the power of

wart und Zukunft ist ja nach Novalis' Ansicht auch charakteristisch für die Dichtkunst, über die er schreibt: «Nichts ist poetischer als Erinnerung und Ahnung oder Vorstellung von der Zukunft. Die gewöhnliche Gegenwart verknüpft Vergangenheit und Zukunft durch Beschränkung. Es gibt aber eine geistige Gegenwart, die beide durch Auflösung identifiziert, und diese Mischung ist das Element, die Atmosphäre des Dichters.»

Die ungewöhnliche Gegenwart der Poesie ist also kein Punkt auf einer ununterbrochen aus der Vergangenheit in die Zukunft sich verlängernden Zeit-Linie, sondern dehnt sich als ästhetisch ausgezeichnete Zeit-Spanne mit der Ideenkraft von Erinnerung und Vorstellung in nicht meßbare Dimensionen aus. Daß sich ein romantischer Dichter im Garten als dem Ort intensiver Eindrücke einer dehnbaren Gegenwart in seinem Element sah, hat vor allem Eichendorff in Lyrik und Prosa zur Sprache gebracht. In seinem Roman «Dichter und ihre Gesellen» gipfelt die Analogie zwischen Garten und Poesie in Fortunats Ausruf: «Was soll ein Garten, wenn er nicht ein Gedicht von ganz bestimmtem Klange ist!» Diese Metapher zielt aufs Ganze der Komposition, worin das «Zugleich» im Garten wie in der Textgestalt eines Gedichts zum Ausdruck kommt. In einer Art simultan-bildhafter, nicht sukzessiv-begrifflicher Sprache tritt hier eine konzentrierte und komplexe Totalität von Zeit- und Ort-, Bild- und Wort-Verknüpfungen in Erscheinung, sowohl verstehbar nach ihrem Sinn als auch wahrnehmbar durch die Sinne. Die Metapher macht darauf aufmerksam, daß die Ästhetik des Gartens mit der des Gedichts konvergiert.

Auf der Ästhetik des Gartens liegt auch die Betonung im gegenwärtigen Gebrauch der Metaphorik der Lesbarkeit überhaupt. Ihre Aktualität gewann sie vor allem als Reaktion auf die Versäumnisse und Übertreibungen einer ökologisch orientierten Planung, die dem Garten zwar die Vielfalt von Natur, aber nicht von Kunst zugesteht.

Beides sucht Dieter Kienast zu verbinden; beispielsweise mit seinem Vorschlag für die Gestaltung des Mechtenbergs und seiner Umgebung im Emschergebiet nach dem «Dornröschen-Prinzip»: umgrenzte, «unberührbare» Orte, von außen als Bau- und Vegetationskörper in der

ideas of memory and imagination into immeasurable dimensions. Above all, Eichendorff expressed in his lyrics and prose how a romantic poet felt in his element in a garden as the place of intensive impressions of a stretchable present. In his novel, "Dichter und ihre Gesellen" (poets and their journeymen), the analogy between garden and poetry culminates in the outcry of Fortunat: "Why a garden if it is not a poem with a specific sound!" This metaphor aims towards the whole of the composition where the "at the same time" in the garden is expressed in the text form of a poem. In a kind of simultaneously-pictorial, not a successively-terminological language, a concentrated and complex totality of time-, location-, picture- and word-connections appears here. It is understandable in its sense – and also perceivable through our senses. The metaphor draws attention to the circumstance that the garden's esthetics converge with those of the poem.

In the contemporary use of the metaphor of readability as such, the tonality lies in the esthetics of the garden. Its actuality was gained above all as a reaction to the neglects and exaggerations of an ecologically oriented planning, allowing into the garden the diversity of nature, but not of art.

Dieter Kienast tries to connect both; for example, with his proposal for the design of the Mechtenberg and its surroundings in the Emsch area following the "sleeping beauty principle": limited "untouchable locations", visible from the outside as building and vegetation volumes, with an undisturbed vegetation "growing in accordance with the earth, light, water and exposition" should be placed according to "landscape design and ecological criteria" and contrast the continual change of the cultural landscape, thus becoming "readable".

Keeping in mind the Bismarck-tower amidst wild rose and boysenberry bushes on the rounded hill-top of the Mechtenberg, Dieter Kienast adds yet another punch-line characteristic of his works to the story of "sleeping beauty 1 – 11". "A poetic opposite is added to the military monument."

Absurdities and contradictions are not merely tolerated by Dieter Kienast in his gardens, but almost elevated to a

Landschaft sichtbar, innen mit einer ungestörten Vegetation «in Übereinstimmung mit Boden, Licht, Wasser und Exposition» bewachsen, sollen nach «landschaftsgestalterischen und ökologischen Kriterien» plaziert werden und die weitere Veränderung der Kulturlandschaft kontrastieren und «damit auch lesbar» machen.

Mit Blick auf den Bismarckturm inmitten verwilderter Rosen- und Brombeerhecken auf der Kuppe des Mechtenberges gewinnt Dieter Kienast der Geschichte von «Dornröschen 1–11» noch eine weitere, für seine Arbeiten charakteristische Pointe ab. «Dem martialischen Denkmal wird ein poetisches Gegenüber beigefügt.»

Ungereimtheiten und Widersprüche werden von Dieter Kienast in seinen Gärten nicht nur toleriert, sondern geradezu zum Gestaltungsprinzip erhoben. Er plädiert für die «Antithese als poetisches Verfahren». Satz und Gegensatz sollen nicht verwischt, entschärft werden, sondern im Kontext ihrer Umgebung deutlich und deutbar zu lesen sein. Natur und Kultur, Wildheit und Domestikation, Weite und Enge, Ferne und Nähe, Weichheit und Härte bilden die dualistischen Figuren, die in seinen Konzepten eine wesentliche Rolle spielen. So beispielsweise im Garten M., wo zwischen den Zeilen von Gesetztem, den aufgereihten Sträuchern, das Gelassene der von selbst gewachsenen Ruderalvegetation als Natur interpretiert werden kann. Kontrast zwischen Geometrie und Wildwuchs, Strengem und Bizarrem kennzeichnet die meisten seiner Gärten, nicht zuletzt den eigenen an der Thujastraße, in dem er seine Autobiographie fortschreibt.

Doch nicht nur metaphorisch, auch wort-wörtlich tritt Geschriebenes in den Gärten auf, die Dieter Kienast und seine Mitarbeiter als «solide Grundlage unserer alltäglichen Arbeit» verstehen. Und vielleicht beruht ja die Tragfähigkeit dieser Grundlage darauf, daß ihr das schöne Gegengewicht der Alltagswelt im Sinn hinter den sinnlich wahrnehmbaren Dingen die Balance hält: Arcadia ist überall, wo sich eine Restfläche ins Imaginäre einer Landschaft weitet, wie sie Vergil, der «Vater des Abendlandes», einst für ein goldenes Zeitalter ganz aus Sprache geschaffen hat.

Als Wort-Ding vergegenwärtigt, ist der altbekannte Topos im Garten am Üetliberg in Zürich für Dieter Kienast

design principle. He pleads for "antithesis as a poetic procedure". Diction and contradiction should not be blotted or disarmed, but should be readable in a clear and interpretable way. Nature and culture, wildness and domestication, width and narrowness, distance and closeness, softness and hardness form the dualistic figures playing an essential role in his concepts. One example is the garden M. where, in between rows of plantings, the lined-up bushes, the untouched places of the ruderal vegetation can be interpreted as nature. The contrast between geometry and wild growth – strict and bizarre – identifies most of his gardens, not the least of which is his own at Thujastrasse, where he continues to write his autobiography.

Written things appear in the gardens, which Dieter Kienast and his collaborators understand as "the solid basis of our daily work", not only metaphorically, but also literally. And maybe the strength of this understanding is based on the circumstance that the beautiful counterweight of the every-day-world in the mind holds the balance behind the sensually perceivable things: Arcadia is wherever a remnant surface widens out into the imaginary of a landscape, as Virgil, the "Father of the occident", had once created for a golden age entirely through the use of language.

Having become present as a 'word-thing', the well-known topos in the garden at Uetliberg in Zurich has become "the strongest narrative element" for Dieter Kienast: "Et in Arcadia ego" – set in concrete letters as a balustrade onto the threshold between the tamed "nature" of the garden and the wildness of the steep wooded slope – at the same time offers a concrete support in and a spiritual enrapture from the material world.

The script as a carrier of meanings for thoughts behind a tangible concrete literacy has also become an image in the garden M. The sentence "Ogni pensiero vola" can be read there from the inside of the garden pavilion and not from the outside, as is the case above the hell's gorge in the sacro bosco of Bomarzo. What does it say in the context of the city, whose center with the "highest church tower in the world" one views beyond the parapet? Does it read like a footnote to the famous history known far beyond this

«zum stärksten narrativen Element» geworden: «Et in Arcadia ego» – in Buchstaben aus Beton als Balustrade auf die Schwelle zwischen der gezähmten «Natur» des Gartens und der Wildnis des steilen Waldhangs gesetzt – bietet handfesten Halt in und spirituelle Entrückung aus der materiellen Welt zugleich.

Schrift als Bedeutungsträger für Gedankliches, das hinter haltbar betonierter Buchstäblichkeit liegt, wird auch im Garten M. zum Bild. Der Satz «Ogni pensiero vola» ist – dort allerdings aus dem Inneren des Gartenpavillons zu lesen, nicht von außen wie über dem Höllenschlund im sacro bosco von Bomarzo. Was sagt er im Kontext der Stadt, auf deren Zentrum mit dem «höchsten Kirchturm der Welt» der Blick über die Brüstung fällt? Liest er sich nicht auch wie eine Fußnote zur weit über diese Stadt hinaus berühmt gewordenen Geschichte vom Schneider und seinem Traum vom Fliegen, die in so vielen Lesarten überliefert ist?

Die Inschrift als trationelles Gartenmotiv kehrt also mit altem Wortlaut, aber dennoch verwandelt zurück. In riesigen Lettern aus einem Guß erscheint Schrift hier sich selbst entfremdet, der Spruch als monumentaler Gegenstand aus gemeinhin verpöntem Beton in Widerspruch zur einstigen poetischen oder mythologischen Bedeutung der Zitate zu treten. Oder erfährt dieses Material als Teil unserer «Wirklichkeiten, die uns nicht immer erquicken», durch die buchstäbliche Verwandlung in einen Start- und Landeplatz für nicht alltägliche Assoziationen eine Nobilitierung?

Gespannt zwischen Kontinuität und Bruch, nimmt das Verhältnis zur Tradition in diesen Gärten nicht nur einander entgegengesetzte, sondern auch ambivalente Formen an. Sie werfen indirekt Fragen auf, die die «Leser» dieser Orte auf ihre Weise, aufgrund ihrer eigenen Geschichte, Sprache und Phantasie unterschiedlich beantworten mögen.

Sich wie Dieter Kienast «mit Lust und Wissen der Gartenkunst anzunehmen», heißt schließlich, «lesen» nicht nur als eine Tätigkeit des Verstandes, sondern vor allem auch der Sinne zu begreifen. Es geht bei dieser Kunst nicht zuletzt darum, den Garten als Spielraum zu lustvoller Entfal-

city of the tailor and his dream of flying which has been handed-down in so many versions?

Thus, the inscription as a traditional garden motif returns with an old phrasing, and yet, transformed. In huge letters made from one cast, the script seems to be estranged from itself. The motto as a monumental object fabricated in the usually disliked concrete material seems to be in opposition to the once poetic or mythological meaning of the quotes. Or is this material, as a part of our "not always refreshing realities", ennobled by the literal transformation into a starting and landing place for unusual associations?

Stretched out between continuity and break, the relationship with tradition in these gardens does not only take on opposing, but also ambivalent forms. They indirectly raise questions to which the "readers" of these locations may respond in their own way, based on their own history, language, and fantasy.

"Taking on the art of gardening with heart and knowledge" as Dieter Kienast has done in the end means finding the ability to understand "reading" not only as an activity of the mind, but, above all, the senses. The point of this art is not in the least to realize and perceive the garden as a playground for the joyful unfolding of all human senses, – including the "sense of possibilities". And perhaps such poetic gardens fulfill – not only in books, but also in reality – a part of the desire which Italo Calvino warmly recommended to us at the end of his "Six suggestions for the next millennium": "If only one work was possible", he wrote, "which would allow us to step out of the limited perspective of an individual ego. Not only to enter into other egos, but to let speak what does not have speech: the bird sitting on the roof gutter, the tree in spring time and the tree in autumn, the stone, the concrete, the plastic material..."

Brigitte Wormbs

tung aller menschlichen Sinne, einschließlich des «Möglichkeitssinnes» auszuführen und wahrzunehmen. Und vielleicht erfüllen solche poetischen Gärten ja nicht nur in Büchern, sondern auch in Wirklichkeit schon etwas von dem Wunsch, den uns Italo Calvino am Schluß seiner «Sechs Vorschläge für das nächste Jahrtausend» ans Herz gelegt hat: «Könnte doch nur ein Werk möglich sein», so schrieb er, «das uns erlauben würde, aus der begrenzten Perspektive eines individuellen Ichs auszutreten, nicht nur, um in andere ähnliche Ichs einzutreten, sondern um sprechen zu lassen, was keine Sprache hat, den Vogel, der sich auf die Dachrinne setzt, den Baum im Frühling und den Baum im Herbst, den Stein, den Beton, den Plastikstoff...»

Brigitte Wormbs

Eintritt in den autobiographischen Garten

Die Autobiographie, diese Hybride aus einer ganz anderen Form der Kunst, erweckt eine seltsame Vorstellung bei einem Garten. Es gibt den Hausgarten, den privaten, intimen und «secreten» Garten, Abstufungen, die einen wachsenden Ausschluß der Betrachter bedeuten. Die intimste Form der Verborgenheit im geheimen Garten gibt den Blick frei, nicht zu einem privaten Inhalt, sondern nur zu einem privaten Raum. Ist das Private nur das Schweigen, das, was nach der Gestaltung kommt? In der Literatur reibt sich das Autobiographische mit der geschlossenen Gestaltung, so das Tagebuch mit dem Roman. Es tritt auf als Antiform, als Bruch mit der Konvention oder dem Tabu, als Quelle des Neuen und Reservat des Anderen. Das Autobiographische ist gewachsener Text, sich verändernde Form, es begleitet die Zeit und es ist offen. Es mißt und begrenzt sich nur gegenüber dem Tod und ruft von dieser Grenze aus nicht nach Ovids «Exegi monumentum», sondern bleibt anarchische Fülle und wendet sich dem Leben zu. Es hat keine Angst vor Aussagen, streift das Cliché, den Kitsch, es zitiert Fremdes, wiederholt Eigenes, es lebt vom Alltag, der Abfallhalde des Verschiedenen und Eigenen. Das Autobiographische betrat die Bühne, als reihum in der Spätmoderne die große Form unter lauter Klage zu Grabe getragen wurde. Für viele blieb das Autobiographische lange eine Ersatzkultur, ein Zeichen der Erschöpfung. Für alle war es jedoch eine Herausforderung. Die Postmoderne hat sich schließlich nur mehr gefreut an diesem ehrenwerten Vorfahren, der bis auf Augustinus zurückgeht. Sie befreit das Autobiographische vom Psychologischen und führt das Private auf den Platz.

Das Autobiographische wird im Garten an der Thujastraße in Zürich auf verschiedenen Ebenen manifest. Es ist zunächst ein Moment der räumlichen Konstellation. Die Stilpluralität ist keine Collage, in der der Heterostil gegenüber dem anderen als different erkannt wird. Die Stilmischung betont hier weniger das Konzeptionelle als vielmehr das Geschichtliche, das Lebensgeschichtliche des

Entering the Autobiographical Garden

The autobiography, this hybrid from a totally different art form, evokes a strange idea when it comes to a garden. There is the house garden, the private garden, the intimate garden, and the "secret" garden, all of which are gradations representing increasingly the exclusion of the observer. The most intimate form of concealment in the secret garden opens up the view to a private space, not a private content. Is privacy just the silence following the design? In literature, the autobiographic creates a friction with the closed concept, as does the diary with the novel. It appears as an anti-form – a break with the convention or the taboo – as a source of the new and repository of the different. The autobiographic is a growing text, a changing form, it accompanies time and is open. It measures and limits itself only towards death, and from this threshold does not call for Ovid's "Exegi monumentum", but remains an anarchic fullness and turns to life. It is not afraid of statements – it touches on the cliché, kitsch; it quotes what is foreign and repeats the individual; it lives from every-day-life, the garbage dump of the different and unique. The autobiography entered the stage when, during the period of late modernism, the large form was buried with loud complaint. For many, the autobiography re-

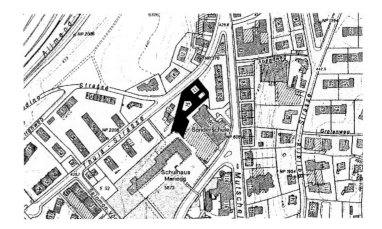

Projektplan 1991
Grundriß
Original 1:100, 84 x 90 cm; Tusche,
Farbstift auf Plandruck

Project plan 1991
Ground plan
Original 1:100, 84 x 90 cm; ink,
color pencil on plan print

Gartens. Die Heterogenität verweist auf die Zeit und nicht auf den Raum. Die Abfolge der Räume gehorcht dem Alltag: der Arbeit, dem Wohnen, dem Ausblick auf die andere Mitwelt. Ältere Räume stehen in späteren, und wenn sie in ihrem Nebeneinander ästhetisch miteinander kommunizieren, ist das freies Spiel, das ihre eigene andere Bedeutung nicht überdeckt, so die autobiographische Erinnerung an Kindheit beim Spielplatz, an Familie im Gewächshaus. Postmoderne Existenz entdeckt sich als Teil einer Familiengeschichte.

Das Tor zur Familiengeschichte öffnet sich in der Kindheit, in unserem Garten in seinem autobiographisch wichtigsten Einzelmotiv, den Tierfiguren. Der Garten gestaltet die Erinnerung an die Kindheit nicht als formales Zeichen, sondern formt den Akt der Erinnerung plastisch nach. Die geschnittenen Baumtiere sind groteske Traumgebilde. Sie überragen alle andern Elemente des Gartens und sind doch nicht vertikale Raumorientierung, sondern erzählte Geschichte, die uns anzieht und die Metamorphose vom Erwachsenen zum Kinde, die sie erzählen, distanzlos miterleben läßt. Wer immer unter diesem phantastischen Federvieh wandert, kommt nicht umhin, weil er zwangsmäßig nach oben schaut, den Kinderblick zu wiederholen, der selbst die kleine Welt des Federviehs von unten sieht, das heißt von so tief unten hinaufschaut, daß der Blick nicht realer Kinderblick ist, sondern in der Erinnerung zu einem Grotesken verschoben wird. Das autobiographische Kind verschwindet in der unendlichen Kleinheit der Imagination.

Mit dieser Metamorphose sind wir vom öffentlichen Raum in den privateren Raum getreten. Der private Raum ist freilich nun nicht der andere Raum, der nach der Metamorphose in das Kind erwartet wird, nicht das Ziel der Metamorphose. Die mythoide Geschichte bleibt als ritueller Akt in sich geschlossen. Die Fabeltiere sind ein Moment des autobiographischen Textes, nicht aber ihre Metageschichte. Der anschließende Raum mit dem Wasserbecken ist streng formal, nicht mehr existentielles, sondern nun mehr ästhetisches Zeichen. Er macht in seiner Abgeschlossenheit, als Raum im Raum, seine Immanenz deutlich und ist in seinem Streben nach Schönheit narzisstisch, ähnlich wie

mained a substitute culture. It was a sign of exhaustion. To all, however, it was a challenge. Post-modernism only took pleasure in this honorable ancestor which goes back to Augustinus. It frees the autobiography from psychology and brings privacy into play.

In the garden at Thujastrasse in Zurich, the autobiographic is apparent on many different levels. First, it is a momentum of spatial constellations. The plurality in style is not a collage in which the hetero-style is recognized as different from the other. The mixture of styles enhances the conceptual less than the historical; i.e., the history of the garden's life. The heterogeneity points to time, not space. The sequence of spaces conforms to every-day-life: work, living, the outlook to the other coexisting world. Older spaces are placed into younger ones. And if they communicate esthetically in their side-by-side coexistence, it is free play which does not disguise different meanings, such as the autobiographic memory of childhood in the playground, and of family in the greenhouse.

The gate to family history opens up during childhood; in our garden it does so with its autobiographically most important single motif, the topiary figures. The garden designs the memory of childhood not as a formal sign, but it sculpturally reshapes the act of memory. The topiary animals are grotesque dream creatures. They surmount all other elements of the garden and yet are not a vertical spatial orientation. They are a narration of history which attracts us and lets us experience the metamorphosis from the adult to the child which they recount without distance. Whoever walks among this fantastic poultry can not help but have the look of a child because they are forced to constantly look up; even the small world of poultry is seen from below, from so far down that the view is not a true child's view, but is shifted into something grotesque in memory. The autobiographic child disappears in the eternal smallness of imagination.

With this metamorphosis we have stepped from the public space into the more private space. Certainly, the private space is not the other space which, succeeding the metamorphosis, is anticipated in the child. This is not the goal of the metamorphosis. The mythogenic story remains

das Baumgeviert gleich nach dem Eingang, in dem auf dem Grund die abwesenden Äpfel in einem abwesenden Spiegel sich rot betrachten. Es sind ästhetische Leer-, besser Pausenzeichen, in deren Formalismus die Nähe zum Zitat spürbar wird. Ausgeformte Gestalt entdeckt sich leichter als Wiederholung, denn singuläre Lebenserfahrung.

Die aufragenden Fabeltiere haben erst im nächsten zentralen Gartenraum ihr Gegenzeichen. Aus dem häuslichen, funktionalen Bereich führen «altväterische» Stufen in die Tiefe. Auf dem Grund verweist abwechselnd mooriges Wasser nicht in helle Höhe, noch dunkle Urtiefe, öffnet sich kein Urauge, das nach innen und nach außen schaut. Die Tiefe verweigert sich, zitiert nicht den artifiziellen Spiegel als ironisches Simulacrum, sondern bleibt bunte, glatte Oberfläche. Plaudern die luftigen Zeichen aus der Kindheit ungehemmt über Bedeutung, verweigert das Zeichen der Tiefe ironisch seine Aussage. Die beiden autobiographischen Symbole sind nicht optisch verbunden, die Beziehung schafft erst die autobiographische Erzählung.

Der Garten endet nicht in der Untiefe, sondern in seiner formal am stärksten herausgearbeiteten Begrenzung, dem Zaun, der die private Erzählung abschließt. Er ist selber schon nicht mehr nur eigener autobiographischer Text, sondern auch fremder, öffentlicher. Noch verweist der Zaun stark auf die andere Umwelt, aber die hoch angelegten Fenster zeigen, daß hier nicht Durchblick, sondern Anblick gemeint sein wird.

Die autobiographische Geschichte ist selber nur ein Moment in der unabgeschlossenen Geschichte. Sie muß immer neu erzählt werden, so wie der Erbauer und das Erbaute in diesem Garten immer neue Geschichten erzählen, ohne daß sie sich aber je ganz aus der Magie der privaten Mythologie werden befreien können und wollen.

German Ritz

closed within itself as a ritual act. The fable animals are a mere moment of the autobiographic text; they are not its meta-history. The adjoining space with the water basin is strictly formal. No longer an existential symbol, it now becomes more of an esthetic one. It clarifies its immanence in its self-contentiousness as a space within the space and, in its striving for beauty, is narcissistic, similar to the square of trees right past the entrance where the non-existent apples watch themselves on the ground in the non-existent mirror. They are esthetic 'pause' symbols in whose formalism the closeness to a quotation becomes perceivable. The well-shaped design discovers itself more easily than repetition or a singular life experience.

The fable animals rising up from the ground receive their counter-symbol only in the following garden space. From the homey functional area, "old grandfather" steps lead into the depths. On the ground, changing moory water does not point into bright heights nor to the darkest age-old depths and no ancient eye opens up to look within, nor out. The depth denies itself. It does not quote the artificial mirror as an ironic simulacrum, but remains a colorful flat surface. Whereas the airy symbols from childhood speak uninhibitedly about meaning, the symbol of depth ironically refuses its statement. The two autobiographic symbols are not linked visually; the relation is created only by the autobiographic story.

The garden does not end in the shallow, but in its formally most strongly worked-out limitation – the fence – which ends the private recitation. It is no longer just its own autobiographic text. It is also a strange and public one. The fence still points to the other environment; however, the high windows show that it is not simply a view that is intended here, but rather a vision.

The autobiographic story is in and of itself only a moment in the unfinished story. It has to be constantly retold in the same way as the builder and the built in this garden constantly tell new stories without, however, ever being able nor wanting to free themselves from the magic of the private mythology.

German Ritz

Die Stilmischung betont hier weniger das Konzeptionelle als vielmehr das Geschichtliche, das Lebensgeschichtliche des Gartens. Die Heterogenität verweist auf die Zeit und nicht auf den Raum.

The mixture of styles enhances the conceptual less than the historical; i.e., the history of the garden's life. The heterogeneity points to time, not space.

Die geschnittenen Baumtiere sind groteske Traumgebilde.
Sie überragen alle andern Elemente des Gartens und sind doch nicht
vertikale Raumorientierung, sondern erzählte Geschichte ...

The topiary animals are grotesque dream creatures.
They surmount all other elements of the garden and yet are not
a vertical spatial orientation. They are a narration of history ...

Der anschließende Raum mit dem Wasserbecken ist streng formal, nicht mehr existentielles, sondern nun mehr ästhetisches Zeichen. Er macht in seiner Abgeschlossenheit, als Raum im Raum, seine Immanenz deutlich und ist in seinem Streben nach Schönheit narzistisch ...

The adjoining space with the water basin is strictly formal. No longer an existential symbol, it now becomes more of an esthetic one. It clarifies its immanence in its self-contentiousness as a space within the space and, in its striving for beauty, is narcissistic ...

Die Tiefe verweigert sich, zitiert nicht den artifiziellen Spiegel als ironisches Simulacrum, sondern bleibt bunte, glatte Oberfläche. Plaudern die luftigen Zeichen aus der Kindheit ungehemmt über Bedeutung ...

The depth denies itself. It does not quote the artificial mirror as an ironic simulacrum, but remains a colorful flat surface. Whereas the airy symbols from childhood speak uninhibitedly about meaning ...

... schon nicht mehr nur eigener autobiographischer Text, sondern auch fremder, öffentlicher. Noch verweist der Zaun stark auf die andere Umwelt, aber die hoch angelegten Fenster zeigen, daß hier nicht Durchblick, sondern Anblick gemeint sein wird.

... no longer just its own autobiographic text. It is also a strange and public one. The fence still points to the other environment; however, the high windows show that it is not simply a view that is intended here, but rather a vision.

Der Kleinste

Unser Aufgabenspektrum erstreckt sich in Maßstabsgrößen von 1:50 bis 1:5'000. Den permanenten Größenwechsel empfinden wir gleichermaßen auf- und anregend. Zunächst sind wir gezwungen, den Fragen des Kontextes und der Angemessenheit unserer Interventionen im Ganzen und im Detail nachzugehen. In kleinen Grundstücken wird dabei das Thema des Kontextes, der nachbarschaftlichen Bezugnahme oder Verweigerung zum generierenden Faktor.

Der Garten liegt in einem größeren, lückig geschlossenen Hof eines Gründerzeitblockes. Er ist eigenständiger Garten und gleichzeitig Teil des Gesamthofraumes. Der Projektplan läßt erkennen, daß mit der umschließenden Kalksandstein-Mauer und der diagonalen Raumgliederung der Kontext des Gesamthofes verweigert wird. Für die Nutzbarkeit erschien uns die deutliche Raumbegrenzung notwendig. Mit Blick auf vorhandene Materialität wurde bei der Ausführung auf die Mauer verzichtet und dafür ein bewachsenes Metallgitter vorgesehen und die Belagsflächen im ortsüblichen Natursteinpflaster ausgeführt. Dieser stärkeren Bezugnahme zum Ort hinsichtlich des Materials steht die unübliche diagonale Raumgliederung gegenüber, mit der die Autonomie dieses kleinsten Gartens

The Smallest

The scale of our projects ranges from 1:50 to 1:5.000. The constant change in size seems exciting and stimulating. First we are forced to look into questions of context and the adequacy of our interventions in the entirety and in the smallest details. In the case of smaller properties, the theme of context, of the reference to the neighbors or the rejection of them, becomes a generating factor.

The garden is located in a larger, incompletely closed courtyard of a block built during the 'Gründerzeit' (years of rapid industrial expansion in Germany). It is an independent garden, while simultaneously it is part of the entire courtyard space. The project plan shows that the context of the entire courtyard is denied by the enclosing cement block wall and the diagonal spatial structure. The clear spatial limitation seemed necessary for usability. Keeping an eye on the existing materials, the realization was accomplished without the wall, and in its place a metal grid covered with plants was installed and the ground was covered with cobble stones as is common in this region. The unusual diagonal spatial structure opposes the stronger reference to the location in terms of material. Thus, the autonomy of this smallest of gardens is enhanced and a stronger depth effect is endeavored. The expressive old cherry tree is apposed by a laterally placed Koelreuteria, forming with its lucid leaves a transparent roof above the garden sitting area. The choice of the low shrubbery and coppice allows for a reaction to the very modest change of sun and shade on the surface.

After ten years, the fence is completely overgrown with ivy and forms a clear spatial limit on a visual level, whereas the tree layer overcomes it and connects with the entire courtyard. Neighbors, such as the pine tree, while appreciated but also less liked, become a self-understood part of this 100 square meter courtyard garden.

Dieter Kienast

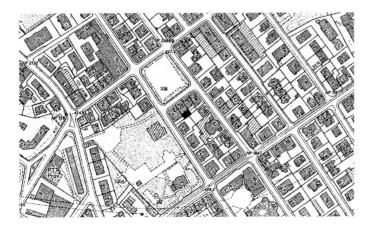

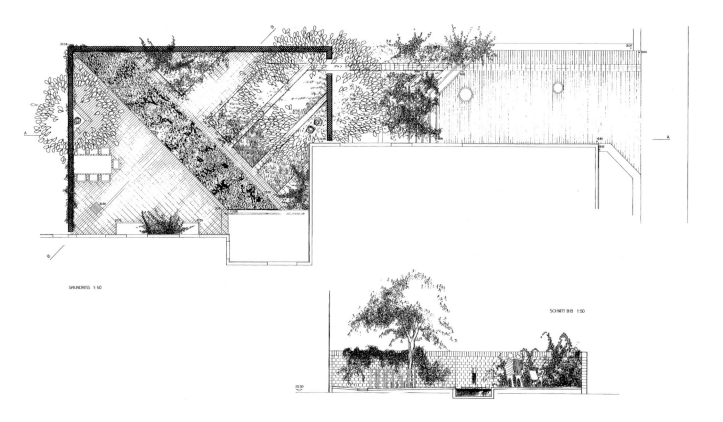

betont und eine stärkere Tiefenwirkung erzielt werden soll. Dem expressiven alten Kirschbaum wird eine seitlich plazierte Koelreuteria gegenübergesetzt, die mit ihren lichten Blättern ein transparentes Dach über dem Gartensitzplatz bildet. Mit der Artenwahl der niedrigen Stauden-Gehölz-Pflanzung wird auf den kleinflächigen Wechsel von Sonne und Schatten reagiert.

Nach zehnjährigem Wachstum ist der Zaun vollständig mit Efeu überwachsen und bildet auf Sichtebene eine deutliche Raumgrenze, während die Baumschicht diese überwindet und sich zum Hofganzen verbindet. Geschätzte, aber auch weniger geliebte Nachbarschaften, wie z.B. die Tanne, werden zum selbstverständlichen Teil dieses 100 m² kleinen Hofgartens.

Dieter Kienast

Projektplan 1982
Grundriß
Original 1:50, 73 x 73 cm;
Tusche auf Lichtpause

Project plan 1982
Ground plan
Original 1:50, 73 x 73 cm;
ink on blueprint

Dieser stärkeren Bezugnahme zum Ort hinsichtlich des Materials steht die unübliche diagonale Raumgliederung gegenüber, mit der die Autonomie dieses kleinsten Gartens betont werden soll ...

The unusual diagonal spatial structure opposes the stronger reference to the location in terms of material. Thus, the autonomy of this smallest of gardens is enhanced ...

Mit der Artenwahl der niedrigen Stauden-Gehölz-Pflanzung wird auf den kleinflächigen Wechsel von Sonne und Schatten reagiert.

The choice of the low shrubbery and coppice allows for a reaction to the very modest change of sun and shade on the surface.

Nach zehnjährigem Wachstum ist der Zaun vollständig mit Efeu überwachsen und bildet auf Sichtebene eine deutliche Raumgrenze, während die Baumschicht diese überwindet und sich zum Hofganzen verbindet.

After ten years, the fence is completely overgrown with ivy
and forms a clear spatial limit on a visual level, whereas the tree layer
overcomes it and connects with the entire courtyard.

Vielfalt und Dichte

Konzept und räumliche Zusammenhänge eines Gartens sind schwer darzustellen. So fällt es nicht leicht, den Garten des Hauses M. als Modell zeitgenössischer Gartenkultur zu begreifen, wenn man nur von Bildern ausgeht. Photographien der Südseite etwa zeigen ein traditionelles Parterre mit Buchseinfassung, das in regelmäßigen Stufen gegen den See hin abbricht. Diese sind ihrerseits mit Buchs vorgepflanzt. Rechts und links führen Treppen zur untersten Gartenebene, die von einem rechteckigen Wasserbecken besetzt ist und talseits von einer geschnittenen Ahornhecke begrenzt wird. Exotische Pflanzen in tönernen Töpfen verschiedenster Art sind vor dem dunkelgrünen Hintergrund der Buchskaskade arrangiert wie die Vasen vor den Brunnenterrassen der Villa d'Este in Tivoli. Der Blick zurück zum efeubewachsenen Haus vermittelt vollends einen Eindruck von Hierarchie, von klassischer Ordnung, eine Ahnung von italienischem Renaissancegarten und von jener Verwunschenheit, die nur ganz alten Orten eigen ist.

Die Erwartungen, welche die Bilder dieses homogenen, auf das Wohnhaus bezogenen Gartenstückes wecken, werden auf der Nordseite enttäuscht. Je nach Blickwinkel ergeben sich hier «malerische», jedenfalls asymmetrisch gefaßte Perspektiven mit ungebändigtem Pflanzenmaterial. Geometrische Elemente – eine platzartige Fläche aus metergroßen Zementplatten, sorgfältig geschnittene Eiben- und Ahornhecken – stehen in lockerer Beziehung zur Eingangsfassade des Hauses. Einige rosa blühende Fuchsien in Töpfen sind frei aufgestellt. Auf den ersten Blick erkennen wir keine logische Entsprechung zum Terrassengarten; es handelt sich offenbar um einen Gartentyp, der als Antithese zum ersten gesehen werden muß, nicht um einen «Naturgarten» allerdings; es könnte, angesichts des sorgfältigen Arrangements, um die Natur als Inszenierung, um eine Demonstration der Künstlichkeit auch eines landschaftlichen Gartens, gehen.

Spätestens jetzt wird es nötig, entweder den Plan zu Rate zu ziehen oder besser – die ganze Anlage abzuschrei-

Variety and Density

The concept and spatial relations of a garden are difficult to represent. Therefore, it is not easy to understand the garden of the M. house as a model of contemporary garden culture on the basis of photographs. For example, the photos of the southern side show a traditional parterre with a frame of box, which break up towards the lake in regular steps. The steps are also framed with box. On the right and left side, steps lead to the lowest garden level which is occupied by a rectangular water basin and limited towards the valley by a trimmed maple hedge. Exotic plants in an assortment of clay pots are arranged in front of the dark green background of the cascade of box like the vases in front of the fountain terraces of Villa d'Este in Tivoli. The view back to the ivy-covered house provides a final impression of hierarchy, of classical order, a sense of Italian Renaissance gardens and of that enchanting aura associated only with very old places.

The expectations raised by the images of this homogeneous piece of garden that refers to the house are let down when attention is turned to the northern side. Depending on the angle, "painterly" images or, at the very least, asymmetrically arranged perspectives with untamed plant material, arise. Geometric elements – a square-like surface

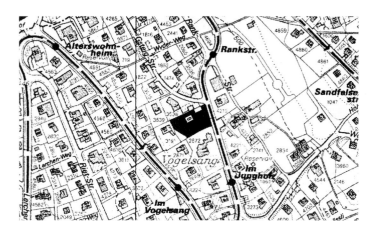

ten. Schon das Haus ist eine Kuriosität: dem symmetrischen Quergiebel gegen den See entspricht auf der Bergseite eine aus der Mitte gerückte, dreieckige Lukarne. Diese bildete einst den Ansatz eines enormen Treibhauses, dessen Grundriß im längsrechteckigen Rasenstück vor dem Haus erhalten ist. Seine Position wurde durch eine parallel angelegte, an die Grundstückgrenze gerückte Remise bestimmt. Was wir heute vor uns haben, ist also lediglich das Fragment einer einst größeren Anlage, des Ökonomiekomplexes einer stattlichen Villa, die auf dem östlichen Nachbargrundstück liegt. Der Eingang des Gärtnerhauses lag ehemals beim Brunnen auf der Ostseite; beim Umbau wurde in jenem Bereich die Bade- und Schlafabteilung angeordnet und die Haustüre in die Achse des ehemaligen Treibhauses versetzt.

Kienast verzichtete nun darauf, den bestehenden Garten umzupflügen, dessen räumliche Ordnung noch auf die Existenz des Glashauses Rücksicht nimmt – wie übrigens auch auf eine Aushöhlung oder einen Neubau des Hauses verzichtet wurde. Bestehende Elemente wie Natursteinmauern und -sitzgelegenheiten wurden im Gegenteil freigelegt und ergänzt. Das rechteckige Rasenstück vor dem neuen Haupteingang erhielt bergseits einen Abschluß in Form einer doppelten Eibenhecke und eine Längenbetonung mit zwei Kugeleiben – räumliche Verstärkungen und Klärungen, die vor allem aus dem Eingangsbereich des Hauses wirksam sind. Dieser Längsentwicklung wurde unmittelbar vor der Fassade eine Querzone in der Form eines plattenbelegten Hartplatzes überlagert, die dem bestehenden Gartenstück eine völlig neue Dimension hinzufügt: den Blick von der mit Mauern und Remise verbauten Westseite – wo ein Sitzplatz geschaffen wurde – hinüber zum hohen Baumbestand gegen die benachbarte Villa hin: ein Blick, der ohne Inszenierung nicht erlebbar wäre. Vor dem ehemaligen Hauseingang beim Brunnen behindert ein erhöhter Vorplatz den unbefugten Zutritt; Kienast schuf hier einen intimen, abgeschlossenen Bereich, dessen Ahornhecke als Gegengewicht zur Remise gedacht ist.

Der Bestand des alten Gartens wird also bewertet, interpretiert, ergänzt und kommentiert. Kienast scheut sich nicht, selbst alte Tannen zu fällen, wenn dies für die

formed by cement paving stones, carefully cut yew and maple hedges – take on a loose relationship with the entrance facade of the house. Some pink-flowering potted fuchsias are freely distributed. At first sight, we can't seem to recognize any logical correspondence with the terrace garden. Obviously, we are dealing here with a garden type that must be seen as the antithesis to the first one, but not with a "natural garden". Given the careful arrangement, it could deal with nature as a production, a demonstration of the artificiality even of a landscaped garden.

Now, at least, it becomes necessary to either consult with the plan, or even better, to actually take a walk through the entire grounds. The house is already a curiosity: the symmetrical cross gable facing the lake is answered on the hillside by a triangular roof-window, placed off-center. It had at one time formed the beginnings of a huge greenhouse whose ground plan is preserved in the longitudinal rectangular piece of lawn in front of the house. Its position was determined by a parallel shed that had been moved to the property border. So, what we see today is merely a fragment of a once larger complex, the outbuildings of a stately villa on the neighboring property to the east. The entrance to the gardener's house was once at the fountain on the east side. During the conversion, the section containing the bathroom and bedroom was placed in this area and the house door was moved to the axis of the former greenhouse.

Kienast then dropped the idea of plowing up the existing garden which, through its spatial order, still considers the existence of the glass house. We also did not want to gut or rebuild the house. On the contrary, many existing elements, such as the natural stone walls and seating areas, were excavated and extended. The rectangular piece of lawn in front of the new main entrance was closed off towards the hill with a yew hedge and longitudinally enhanced with two sphere-shaped yews – spatial clarifications which have their greatest effect, above all, when viewed from the entrance area of the house. Immediately in front of the facade, this longitudinal development was overlapped by a transverse-zone in the form of a tile-covered court, adding a completely new dimension to the ex-

Projektpläne 1989
Grundriß und Schnitte
Originale 1:100, 58 x 95 cm;
Bleistift und Farbstift
auf grauem Halbkarton

Project plans 1989,
Ground plan and sections
Originals 1:100, 58 x 95 cm;
pencil and colored pen
on gray illustration board

Klärung der Raumbildung notwendig ist. Wenige wichtige Bäume werden belassen, schöne Exemplare – etwa ein Magnolienbaum – freigestellt. Die Eingriffe zielen darauf, Vorhandenes nicht abzuschotten, sondern aufzudecken und einzubeziehen. So zeigt dieser nördliche Gartenteil exemplarisch, wie mit Fragmenten gearbeitet werden kann. Bestehendes, mit kleinen Eingriffen ergänzt, erhält einen neuen Sinn, der zwar das Ganze umfaßt, nicht aber auf eine «Totale Architektur», auf die «Unverfrorenheit und Unzweideutigkeit» eines alles umfassenden Wurfes abzielt. Rowe und Koetter, die mit Recht die Architektur der Gärten als Kritik an der Architektur der Stadt auffassen[1], stellen in diesem Zusammenhang das Konzept von Versailles dem Modell der Villa Hadriana gegenüber. Deren «relativierend inszenierte Stücke» sind Musterbeispiele eines stückweise vorgeführten, komplexen, von Reminiszenzen bestimmten Entwurfes. Auch Kienast verwendet die Verfahren des «Weiterstrickens», des lokalen Eingriffes, der Überlagerung, der Collage. Es ist evident, daß er dabei seinerseits einem Muster folgt, das sich etwa 1965 in der Architektur- und Städtebaudiskussion abzuzeichnen begann und das sich – wenigstens in der Theorie – seither weitgehend durchgesetzt hat. Aus dieser Sicht gewinnt unser Garten eine erste Stufe von Aktualität und von Bedeutung.

Die stilistischen Mittel, die Kienast einsetzt, stützen sich vor allem auf den Kontrast von organisch bestimmter, freier Form zur geometrischen Setzung des Menschen. Diese umfaßt nicht nur das Gebaute, sondern auch Pflanzenmaterial, das gezähmt, geschnitten, künstlich in geometrische Form gebracht wird. Im großen Maßstab wird der geometrische Nahbereich des Hauses, der sich auf der Westseite an die baulich definierte Kante anlehnt, ausgespiegelt gegen die großzügige Baumkulisse, die zur «Verbergung der Grenzen» gegen den Garten der Villa hin dient (ein Begriff, den Peter Joseph Lenné bei der Beschreibung englischer Landschaftsgärten verwendet hat[2]). Im Kleinen wird das Prinzip etwa bei den Fugen der Zementplatten lesbar, die mit Duftkräutern ausgepflanzt sind: diese Pflanzen entwickeln sich, der Benützung des Platzes folgend, in der unregelmäßigen Geometrie des Fugennetzes.

isting piece of garden: the view from the west side built-in with walls and the shed where a seating area was created to the high trees and the neighboring villa; a view which could not be experienced without this development. In front of the former house entrance at the fountain, a raised entry court prevents unauthorized access; Kienast has created an intimately enclosed area here, whose maple hedge is thought of as a counterweight to the shed.

The population of the old garden is thus qualified, interpreted, extended and commented on. Kienast does not shy away from cutting down even the old pine trees if it's necessary for clarifying the spatial form. Only a few important trees are left standing. The most beautiful ones are liberated. One example would be the wonderful magnolia tree. The operations aim not at sealing off the existing, but at uncovering and integrating it. Thus, this northern part of the garden shows in an exemplary way how one can work with fragments. The existing, complemented with small operations, receives a new meaning which embraces the whole yet does not aim at an "unambiguous and unabashed" "total architecture" or of an all-embracing strike. Rowe and Koetter, who justifiably understand the garden architecture as a criticism of the urban architecture[1], compare, in this context, the concept of Versailles with the model of the Villa Hadriana. Its "relativistically produced 'bits'" are perfect examples of a partially staged, complex design determined by recollections. Kienast also uses the procedures of a further 'knitting together' of the local operation – the overlapping; the collage. It is evident that he follows a pattern which began to evolve in the architectural and urban architectural discussion from around 1965 which, at least theoretically, has asserted itself widely ever since. From this perspective, our garden gains a primary level of actuality and importance.

The stylistic means used by Kienast are based above all on the contrast of organically determined free form and the geometric placements by humans. This not only includes the buildings, but also the plant material which is trimmed, tamed and brought into an artificial geometric form. On a large scale, the close proximity of the house, which leans onto the architecturally defined edge on the

Für seine baulichen Setzungen verwendet Kienast gerne Sichtbeton oder Zementwaren. Einerseits handelt es sich dabei um ein «armes» Material, dessen Oberflächenqualität nicht von der reinen Form ablenkt (Le Corbusier propagierte schon 1921 die «matériaux bruts» als Mittel zur Erzeugung von räumlichen Gebilden, die den Betrachter zutiefst bewegen[3]). Andererseits ist der Beton ein Baustoff, der zur Moderne gehört und eine zeitliche Zuordnung der neuen Eingriffe erlaubt (daher die Einfassung der Natursteinpfläserung vor dem Badezimmer). In dieser Beziehung haben es ja die Landschaftsarchitekten schwer: Ihr primärer Baustoff bleibt sich immer gleich, und auch die mit dem Pflanzenmaterial erzielbaren räumlichen Wirkungen sind längst erprobt – kein Wunder, daß Kienast «architektonischen» Formulierungen seines Gartens viel Aufmerksamkeit widmet.

Es lohnt sich nun, auch die Südseite, die uns zunächst als traditionelle, fast nostalgisch wirkende Oase erschien, auf die erwähnten Merkmale hin zu überprüfen. Hier ist anzumerken, daß Katharina Medici, eine gelehrte und passionierte Gartenliebhaberin, selbst das obere Gartenparterre mit den fünf von Buchshecken eingefaßten Staudenbeeten angelegt hat. Diese bilden also den «point de départ» für die weitere Arbeit. In die Böschung mit verwilderter Bepflanzug, die vor der Gartenumänderung zur Grundstücksgrenze vermittelte, wurden drei Stufen und eine Terrasse eingeschnitten, die mit Splitt belegt und wiederum mit Zementwaren begrenzt sind. Das elegante Wasserbecken auf der untersten Ebene ist ebenfalls mit schmalen Betonelementen eingefaßt. Es bildet von oben her gesehen den Abschluß des Gartens, einen horizontalen Spiegel, der hinführt zur breit gelagerten Perspektive des Zürichsees. Von unten gesehen führt es das Spiel mit Querbezügen weiter, die diesen Garten als Ganzes prägen: es verleiht dem Blick zur seitlichen Baumkulisse hin eine präzise Richtung und macht wiederum aufmerksam auf das Verfahren des Kontrastes, das auch diesem Grundstück zugrunde liegt.

Der Terrassengarten erscheint somit als Verstärkung eines bereits vorhandenen Fragmentes. Die Wahl dieses Typs ist aber auch von der Notwendigkeit her zu erklären,

west side, is reflected against the generous tree scenery serving the "concealment of the borders" towards the garden of the villa (this is a term used by Peter Joseph Lenné when describing the English landscape gardens[2]). On a small scale, the principle can be read; e.g., in the seams of the cement tiles which are filled with scented herbs: these plants develop following the irregular geometry of the seam network.

For his constructive placements, Kienast likes to use fair-faced concrete or cement-wares. On one hand, the surface quality of this "poor" material does not distract from the pure form (in 1921, Le Corbusier had already propagated the "matérieaux bruts" as a means of creating spatial structures which deeply move the observer[3]). On the other hand, concrete is a building material which belongs to modernism and allows a chronological assignment of the new operations (therefore the framing of the natural stone tiles outside the bathroom). In this respect, the landscape architects are having a difficult time: their primary building material always remains the same and the spatial effects which can be created with the plant material have long ago been tried out – it is no surprise that Kienast devotes a lot of attention to the "architectural" composition of his garden.

It is now worth checking out the south side for the aforementioned characteristics, as it appeared at first to be a traditional and almost nostalgic oasis. At this point, it should be mentioned that Katharina Medici, herself an educated and passionate garden lover, laid out the upper garden parterre with the five shrub beds framed by box. These form the "starting point" for the further work. Three steps and a terrace covered with gravel and framed with cement ware were cut into the wildly overgrown slope which, before the change of the garden, mediated towards the property border. The elegant water basin on the lowest level is also framed with small concrete elements. Seen from above, it forms the enclosure of the garden, a horizontal mirror leading to the broad view of Lake Zurich. Seen from below, it continues the play with cross references which mark this garden as a whole: it provides the view of the lateral tree scenery with a precise direction and again points

die Vielfalt der südlichen Pflanzen aus der Sammlung der Hausherrin zusammenzufassen und in einen größeren Zusammenhang einzubinden. Die Freude an der Exotik dieser Pflanzen ist zwar Bestandteil der Gartenkultur; deren unbedachte Verteilung im Garten führt aber zum Widerspruch mit dem Postulat, vom Charakter eines Ortes – letztlich von der Landschaftlichkeit – auszugehen und diesen zu verstärken. Durch die Geometrisierung der Terrassen erhält die Pflanzensammlung einen Rahmen und eine präzise Rolle im Plan des Gartens zugewiesen.

Zwei gegensätzliche Gartenstile finden sich also auf engstem Raum: auf den ersten Blick fast zuviel des Guten. Kienast meint aber, daß sich der Besitz eines Ortes nicht über die Grundstücksgröße definiert, sondern über die Intensität der Auseinandersetzung mit diesem Ort[4]. Von daher wird die Vision von Dichte erklärbar, die das Konzept des Gartens ausmacht – Dichte nicht aus formaler, sondern zuerst aus inhaltlicher Begründung heraus. Zur Erzeugung von Vielfalt wird die Methode sowie Kontrastierung auf doppelte Weise eingesetzt: Maximale Geometrisierung im Westen (im Bereich des Hauses) versus maximale Freiheit in den östlichen Bereichen (beim Wäldchen an der Grenze zur Villa hin); asymmetrische Komposition und «Landschaftsgarten» im Norden gegen symmetrischen Aufbau und «geometrischen Terrassengarten» im Süden. Dabei entpuppt sich die Antithese als poetisches Verfahren, als Möglichkeit, nicht nur Vielfalt zu erzeugen, sondern auch dem Umgang mit der Natur ein geistiges Vergnügen abzugewinnen.

Daß man auf derart souveräne Weise mit allen möglichen Ausdrucksformen der Gartenkunst umgehen kann, ist relativ neu. Allzu oft erschienen während der letzten Jahrzehnte geometrische Elemente – etwa das ominöse «Bauerngärtlein» – als bloße nostalgische Versatz- und Dekorationsstücke ohne jede Verankerung und Funktion im räumlichen Konzept des betreffenden Ortes. Der Verlust an diesbezüglichem Wissen ließ sich bis in die Technik der Plandarstellung von Gartenprojekten hinein verfolgen. Es ist das Verdienst von Leuten wie Kienast, an die große Tradition der Gartenkunst wieder anzuknüpfen, ohne die überlieferten Elemente zu Versatzstücken abzuwerten.

out the process of contrast which is the basis of this property.

Thus, the terrace garden appears as a reinforcement of an already existing fragment. The choice of this type, however, can also be explained through the necessity of summarizing the variety of southern plants from the lady of the house's collection and integrating it into a larger context. The joy in the exoticness of these plants may be a component of garden culture; however, their thoughtless distribution in the garden leads to a contradiction of the postulate of taking the character of a location – in the end, the landscape – as a starting point, and then to enhance it. By making the terraces geometric, the collection of plants is provided with a framework and precise role in the plan of the garden.

Two opposing garden styles, at first sight and in such a small area, seem to be almost too much. Kienast, however, feels that the richness of a place does not define itself by the size of the property, but by the intensity of preoccupation with this location.[4] Thus, the vision of density which defines the concept of the garden becomes explicable – density not for a formal reason, but, first and foremost, for a contextual reason. In order to create variety, method and contrast are used in two ways: a maximum of geometry in the west (in the vicinity of the house) versus a maximum of freedom in the eastern areas (close to the small forest towards the border of the villa); an asymmetrical composition and "landscape garden" in the north versus the symmetrical design and "geometric terrace garden" in the south. The antithesis turns out to be a poetic procedure; a possibility to not only create variety, but also to provide the handling of nature with a spiritual pleasure.

It is a relatively new thing to handle all possible expressive forms of the art of gardening in such a sovereign way. During the past few decades, geometric elements have appeared much too often – such as the ominous "small farmer's garden" – merely as nostalgic theatrical sets and decorative pieces without any roots or function in the spatial concept of the appropriate location. The loss of this kind of knowledge could be followed up to the technique of representing plans for garden projects. It is the ac-

complishment of people like Kienast to reconnect to the big tradition of the art of gardening without degrading the inherited elements into these theatrical sets. History is not viewed as an exploitable warehouse whose elements can be used and manipulated at will. Instead, the exact knowledge of the basic ideas in the art of gardening allows for the recognition of found objects and providing them with an adequate value in a new, denser and more exciting composition through a process that asks, however, for sacrifices in the existing population. Thus, a story which had begun long ago indeed can be continued sensibly. On this level, the small garden of the M. house fulfills the promise by Rowe and Koetter to gain ideas from garden architecture for urban architecture.[5]

Arthur Rüegg

1 Colin Rowe, Fred Koetter, Collage City, Cambridge Mass. and London 1978
2 See also Gerhard Heinz, Peter Joseph Lenné, Göttingen 1977, p. 21
3 In "L'Esprit Nouveau". See Le Corbusier, Vers une architecture, Paris 1923
4 Dieter Kienast, Die Sehnsucht nach dem Paradies, in: Hochparterre 7/1990
5 See Kienast's successful competition project for the design of Waisenhausplatz and Bärenplatz in Bern, 1990

Das rechteckige Rasenstück vor dem neuen Haupteingang erhielt bergseits einen Abschluß in Form einer doppelten Eibenhecke und eine Längenbetonung mit zwei Kugeleiben ...

The rectangular piece of lawn in front of the new main entrance was closed off towards the hill with a yew hedge and longitudinally enhanced with two sphere-shaped yews ...

Die Eingriffe zielen darauf, Vorhandenes nicht abzuschotten, sondern aufzudecken und einzubeziehen.

The operations aim not at sealing off the existing, but at uncovering and integrating it.

... das Spiel mit Querbezügen weiter, die diesen Garten als Ganzes prägen: es verleiht dem Blick zur seitlichen Baumkulisse hin eine präzise Richtung und macht wiederum aufmerksam auf das Verfahren des Kontrastes ...

... the play with cross references which mark this garden as a whole: it provides the view of the lateral tree scenery with a precise direction and again points out the process of contrast ...

... unmittelbar vor der Fassade eine Querzone, in der Form
eines plattenbelegten Hartplatzes überlagert, die dem bestehenden
Gartenstück eine völlig neue Dimension hinzufügt ...

Immediately in front of the facade, this longitudinal development
was overlapped by a transverse-zone in the form of a tile-covered court,
adding a completely new dimension to the existing piece of garden ...

Exotische Pflanzen in tönernen Töpfen verschiedenster Art
sind vor dem dunkelgrünen Hintergrund der Buchskaskade arrangiert
wie die Vasen vor den Brunnenterrassen der Villa d'Este in Tivoli.

Exotic plants in an assortment of clay pots are arranged in front
of the dark green background of the cascade of box like the vases in front of
the fountain terraces of Villa d'Este in Tivoli.

An Stelle des Bauernhofes

Umnutzungen sind zu einem bedeutenden Aspekt im planerischen Alltag geworden. Im geläufigen Planerjargon Konversion genannt, werden Kasernen in Kulturhäuser verwandelt, alte Fabrikareale zu Technologiezentren entwickelt und Landwirtschaftsflächen zu Golfplätzen oder Reiterhöfen umfunktioniert. Mit der Umwandlung ist immer eine Nobilitierung des Standortes verbunden, die Wertschöpfung muß intensiviert und angepaßt werden. Der großflächige Umbau unserer Landschaft infolge aufgegebener Landwirtschaftsflächen wird deshalb ein zentrales Thema unserer Landschaftsplanung werden.

Im kleinsten Maßstab ist auch das vorliegende Projekt mit dem Thema der Konversion verbunden. Etwas gegen den Strich gebürstet, steht hier nicht die Steigerung, sondern die Verweigerung der Wertschöpfung zur Diskussion.

Wir sind weit draußen in der Ostschweiz, in einem kleinen Weiler außerhalb von Amriswil. Ein Konglomerat von «echten» Landwirtschaftshöfen und umgenutzten Bauernhöfen. Zu letzteren gehört auch unser prächtiger Bauernhof, in dem zwei Familien wohnen. Gegen Süden ans offene Feld grenzend, ist die Aussicht beeindruckend – auf Obstwiesen und dahinter auf die leicht gebrochene Idylle eines Silohochhauses und der appenzellischen Voralpenlandschaft. Wir wenden uns nicht dem Haus und Garten, sondern dem östlichen Nachbargrundstück zu, auf dem ein kleines Bauernhaus stand, eingewachsen in eine zehnjährige Wildnis. Das Grundstück hatten unsere Besitzer gekauft, um zukünftig allzu nahe Nachbarschaften zu vermeiden. Nachdem das Gebäude unter der Schneelast zusammengestürzt war, stellte sich die luxuriöse Frage nach dem Sinn und Gebrauch des Grundstückes, das eigentlich nicht gebraucht wird. Die bescheidenen Wünsche nach einem größeren Sitzplatz und einigen Gemüsebeeten erschienen kaum raumfüllend für ein Grundstück von 1500 m² Größe.

Zweierlei Einsichten ergab die Analyse vor Ort: Aufgrund der Lage und Ausrichtung des großen Hauses und

Instead of the Farm

Re-utilization has become an important aspect in the every-day-life of planners. Called 'conversion' in the current planners' lingo, barracks are transformed into cultural centers, old factory areas are developed into technological centers, and agricultural areas are turned into golf courses or horse farms. The conversion always involves an ennobling of the location; the profitability must be intensified and adapted. The large scale conversion of our landscape due to the abandonment of agricultural areas will therefore become a central theme in our landscape planning.

On the smallest scale, the project which we are discussing here is also related to the theme of conversion. In this case though, and against all odds, it is not the increase, but rather the refusal of profitability which is to be discussed.

We are out in eastern Switzerland, in a small hamlet outside of Amriswil, a conglomerate of "true" agricultural farms and converted farms. Our gorgeous farm is among the latter, and two families live on it. Bordering the open

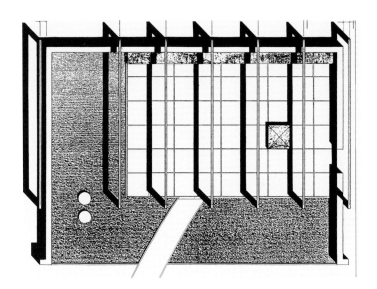

Detailplan Sitzplatz 1991
Grundriß
Original 1:50, A3

Detailed plan of sitting area, 1991
Ground plan
Original 1:50, A3

der zwei Grundstücke ist eine Erweiterung des bestehenden Gartens weder sinnvoll noch möglich. So wird das neue Grundstück zu einem räumlich getrennten, eigenständigen Gartenteil entwickelt. Zum Zweiten erweist sich die Lage des alten Gebäudes als dorfräumlich ideal für die Situierung des Sitzplatzes.

Die Grundfläche des alten Hauses wird dreiseitig durch eine Mauer gefaßt und somit Räumlichkeit im Straßen- und Gartenbereich wieder hergestellt. Eine einfache Eisen-/Holzkonstruktion überspannt den Platz und verstärkt seine Raumhaltigkeit. Die L-förmige Quarzsandfläche bildet die Zäsur zwischen Sitzplatz und Gartenland und verweist auf den alten Gebäudeboden. Die vegetationslose Sandfläche kontrastiert mit der üppig nachwachsenden Schuttvegetation und dem großflächigen Staudenbeet zwischen altem und neuem Garten. Zwei kleine, runde Wasserbecken mit schwimmenden Wasserlinsen treten mit dem künstlich wirkenden Hellgrün aus dem fahlen Gelb des Sandes heraus.

So wird Konversion nicht nur in der Nutzung, sondern auch in der räumlichen Auffassung und in der Pflanzenverwendung fortgeschrieben. Das jetzt gegen vorne und oben offene Haus wird zum Eß-, Ruhe- und Aussichtsplatz auf Garten und Landschaft. Im Garten vereint sind drei prototypische Arten des Vegetationsbewuchses: Das Wilde, das Nützliche und das Schöne:

- die sich selbst entwickelnde Ruderalvegetation beim Sitzplatz erinnert an die aufgegebene bäuerliche Nutzung und signalisiert die Wertschätzung der früher als Unkraut diffamierten, naturgewachsenen Vegetation, die damit auch einen neuen Bedeutungsgehalt bekommen hat.
- Gemüsebeete und Kompostierung stehen für den intensivst genutzten Gartenteil, der sich in diese Umgebung nahtlos integriert.
- Zwischen Bogenweg und interner Westgrenze ist ein großflächiges Staudenbeet angelegt. Form, Größe und Pflanzenverwendung verweigern sich dem Typus des historisierenden Bauerngartens. Das Farbenspektrum bleibt im blauen und weißen Farbton. Die Flieder-

field in the south the view is impressively directed towards orchards and, beyond the slightly disturbed ideal of a silo-like high rise building and the foothills of the Appenzell Alps. We will turn our attention not to the farm house and garden, but to the neighboring property to the east where there once was a small farm house in the midst of a wilderness that had been growing over a period of ten years. The owners had bought the property in order to circumvent any future development of the land in the immediate neighborhood. After the building had collapsed under the weight of snow, the luxurious question of the sense and use of this property that was not really needed was raised. The modest wish for a larger outdoor sitting area and a few vegetable borders hardly seems adequate to fill the space of the 1500 square meter lot.

The on-site diagnosis brought about two insights. Given the location and orientation of the large house and the two properties, an extension of the existing garden is neither sensible nor possible. Thus, the new property will be developed into a spatially separate garden. Secondly, the location of the old building seems to be ideal in a village-related context for the situation of the sitting area.

The base of the old house will be enclosed by a wall on three sides and, thus, a spatial relationship with the street and garden areas will be reestablished. A simple iron and wood construction covers the area and enhances its spatial quality. The L-shaped quartz sand area forms the caesura between the sitting area and garden and refers to the old building's floor. The sand surface, lacking vegetation, contrasts with the richly regrowing ruderal vegetation and the large scale shrubbery border between the old and the new garden. Two small, round water basins with floating water lenses emerge with the seemingly artificial light green from the pale yellow of the sand.

In this way, conversion is continued not only in the utilization, but also in the spatial approach and the use of plants. The house, which is now opened towards the front and top, has become a place for eating, relaxing and for viewing the garden and landscape. Three archetypes of vegetation are united in the garden: the wild, the useful and the beautiful:

Weißes Beet
Achillea ptarmica 'Boule de Neige'
Alchemilla mollis
Anemone japonica 'H. Jobert'
Anemone silvestris grandiflora
Angelica archangelica
Artemisia lactiflora
Asperula odorata
Astrantia major
Digitalis lutea
Digitalis purpurea alba
Geranium pratense 'Kashmir White'
Helleborus corsicus
Helleborus foetidus
Helleborus niger
Lysimachia clethroides
Malva moschata alba
Meconopsis cambrica
Myrrhis odorata
Omphalodes verna alba
Phlomis samia
Polygonatum multiflorum
Tellima grandiflora
Thalictrum glaucum
Verbascum 'Gainsborough'
Vinca minor 'G. Jekyll'

Flieder Beet
Aconitum carmichaelii 'fischeri'
Anemone hupehensis 'Splendens'
Aquilegia alpina 'Superba'
Aster frikartii 'Mönch'
Aster frikartii 'Wunder von Stäfa'
Aster novi-belgii 'Royal Velvet'
Aster novi-belgii 'Schöne von Dietlikon'
Baptisia australis
Campanula lactiflora
Campanula latifolia
Campanula persicifolia 'Bläuling'
Centaurea montana
Delphinium belladonna 'Piccolo'
Dicentra spectabilis
Echinops ritro 'Veitchs Blue'
Gaura lindheineri
Geranium 'Johnsons Variety'
Geranium 'Rose Clair'
Geranium 'Russell Prichard'
Geranium endressii
Geranium nodosum
Geranium oxonianum 'Claridge Druce'
Geranium platypetalum
Geranium wallichianum
Gidalcea hybr. 'Elsie Hengh'
Hesperis matronalis
Hosta ventricosa
Hyssopus aristatus
Hyssopus officinalis
Knautia macedonia
Lavandula officinalis 'Hidcote Blue'
Lavatera 'Barnsley'
Linaria purpurea
Linaria purpurea 'C. Want'
Lobelia vedranriensis
Lobelia vedranriensis 'Siphilitica'
Lupinus 'Edelknabe'
Lupinus polyphyllus (blau)
Malva moschata
Nepeta mussinii
Paeonia lactiflora 'Henri Potin'
Phlox maculata 'Omepa'
Phlox maculata 'Rosalinde'
Phlox paniculata 'E. Arden'
Polemonium caeruleum
Rosmarinus officinalis
Salvia officinalis 'purpurascens'
Salvia nemorosa 'Blauhügel'
Stachys grandiflora
Thalictrum aquilegifolium
Veronica longifolia 'Blauriesin'
Veronica spicata 'Rotfuchs'
Veronica virginica
Viola labradorica

White border
Achillea ptarmica 'Boule de Neige'
Alchemilla mollis
Anemone japonica 'H. Jobert'
Anemone silvestris grandiflora
Angelica archangelica
Artemisia lactiflora
Asperula odorata
Astrantia major
Digitalis lutea
Digitalis purpurea alba
Geranium pratense 'Kashmir White'
Helleborus corsicus
Helleborus foetidus
Helleborus niger
Lysimachia clethroides
Malva moschata alba
Meconopsis cambrica
Myrrhis odorata
Omphalodes verna alba
Phlomis samia
Polygonatum multiflorum
Tellima grandiflora
Thalictrum glaucum
Verbascum 'Gainsborough'
Vinca minor 'G. Jekyll'

Lilac border
Aconitum carmichaeli 'fischeri'
Anemone hupehensis 'Splendens'
Aquilegia alpina 'Superba'
Aster frikartii 'Monk'
Aster frikartii 'Miracle of Stäfa'
Aster novi-belgii 'Royal Velvet'
Aster novi-belgii 'Beauty of Dietlikon'
Baptisia australis
Campanula lactiflora
Campanula latifolia
Campanula persicifolia 'Bläuling'
Centaurea montana
Delphinium belladonna 'Piccolo'
Dicentra spectabilis
Echinops ritro 'Veitchs Blue'
Gaura lindheineri
Geranium 'Johnsons Variety'
Geranium 'Rose Clair'
Geranium 'Russel Prichard'
Geranium endressii
Geranium nodosum
Geranium oxonianum 'Claridge Druce'
Geranium platypetalum
Geranium wallichianum
Gidalcea hybr. 'Elsie Hengh'
Hesperis matronalis
Hosta ventricosa
Hyssopus aristatus
Hyssopus officinalis
Kanutia macedonia
Lavandula officinalis 'Hidcote Blue'
Lavatera 'Barnsley'
Linaria purpurea
Linaria purpurea 'C. Want'
Lobelia vedranriensis
Lobelia vedranriensis 'Siphilitica'
Lupinus 'Noble Boy'
Lupinus polyphyllus (blue)
Malva moschata
Nepeta mussinii
Paeonia lactiflora 'Henri Potin'
Phlox maculata 'Omepa'
Phlox maculata 'Rosalinde'
Phlox paniculata 'E. Arden'
Polemonium caeruleum
Rosmarinus officinalis
Salvia officinalis 'purpurascens'
Salvia nemorosa 'Blue Hill'
Stachys grandiflora
Thalictrum aquilegifolium
Veronica longifolia 'Blue Giantess'
Veronica spicata 'Red fox'
Veronica virginica
Viola labradorica

Pflanzliste Staudenbeete

Planting list in the shrubbery borders

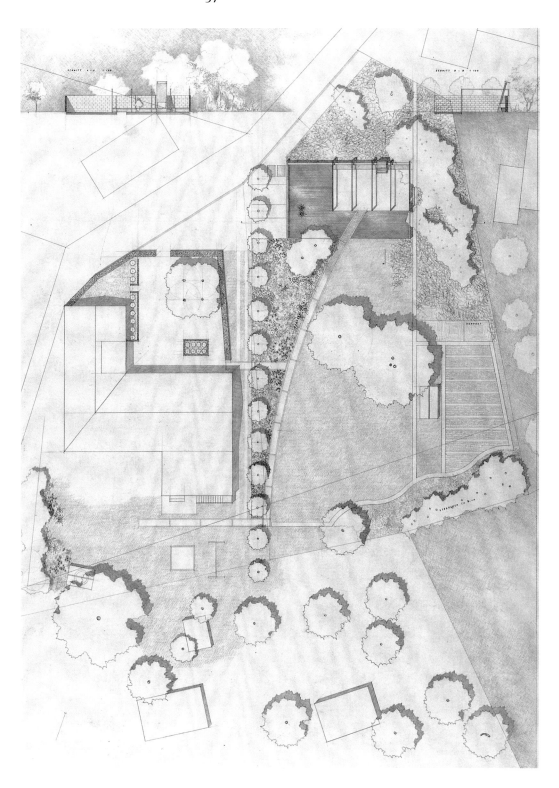

Projektplan 1989
Grundriß und Schnitte
Original 1:100, 66 x 97 cm; Bleistift
auf grauem Halbkarton

Project plan 1989
Ground plan and sections
Original 1:100, 66 x 97 cm; pencil
on gray semi-cardboard

hochstammreihe markiert die transparente, räumliche Grenze zum Wohnhaus und wechselt von blau zu weiß. Stauden und Kleinsträucher variieren in Blattformen und fein aufeinander abgestimmten Farbtönen.

Die differenzierten, vielfältigen Pflanzenvorkommen und die ungewohnten Raumdefinitionen lassen den Garten als gleichzeitig vertraut und fremd erscheinen. Er ist weder Bauern- noch Einfamilienhausgarten und nähert sich als eigenständiger Typus dem von den Architekten Rausser & Clemençeau umgebauten Bauernhaus, dessen Inneres im spannungsvollen Kontrast zum weitgehend unverändert belassenen, rustikalen Äußeren steht.

Dieter Kienast

- the ruderal vegetation at the sitting area reminds one of the abandoned agricultural function of the area and signifies the appreciation of the indigenous vegetation which, in the past, was maligned as being weeds and has now obtained a new meaning;
- vegetable borders and compost heaps represent the most intensively used part of the garden, which is integrated seamlessly into this environment;
- between the curved pathway and the internal western border, a large bush border was laid out. Form, size and plantings reject the category of the historic farmer's garden. The range of colors stays within the blue and the white. The row of high lilac trees marks the transparent, spatial border to the house and changes from blue to white. Bushes and small shrubs vary in the forms of their leaves and subtly harmonized shades of color.

The diversified plantings and the unusual spatial definitions make the garden appear both familiar and strange at the same time. It is neither a farmer's garden nor a single-family home garden and, as an individual type, approaches the farm house whose interior, excitingly renovated by the architects Rausser & Clemençeau, stands in suspenseful contrast with the rustic outside which, for the most part, has been preserved.

Dieter Kienast

Die L-förmige Quarzsandfläche bildet die Zäsur zwischen
Sitzplatz und Gartenland und verweist auf den alten Gebäudeboden.
Die vegetationslose Sandfläche kontrastiert ...

The L-shaped quartz sand area forms the caesura
between the sitting area and garden and refers to the old building's floor.
The sand surface, lacking vegetation, contrasts ...

... die sich selbst entwickelnde Ruderalvegetation beim Sitzplatz erinnert an die aufgegebene bäuerliche Nutzung und signalisiert die Wertschätzung der früher als Unkraut diffamierten, naturgewachsenen Vegetation ...

... the ruderal vegetation at the sitting area reminds one of the abandoned agricultural function of the area and signifies the appreciation of the indigenous vegetation which, in the past, was maligned as being weeds ...

Die Grundfläche des alten Hauses wird dreiseitig durch eine Mauer gefaßt und somit Räumlichkeit im Straßen- und Gartenbereich wieder hergestellt.

The base of the old house will be enclosed by a wall on three sides and, thus, a spatial relationship with the street and garden areas will be reestablished.

Zürcher Geschichten
Garten Villa Wehrli in Zürich

Hans Waldmanns Denkmal mit Roß und Reiter steht – etwas beiläufig im wörtlichen Sinne – am Brückeneck der Limmat. Städtebaulich zurückhaltend, mit betonter Bescheidenheit in Situierung und Dimension verrät es Eigenarten der Stadt Zwinglis, der Stadt der Zünfter und der Wirtschaft. Der Kondottiere Waldmann war durch Kriegs- und Wirtschaftserfolg rasch zum Renaissance-Potentaten von unschweizerischer Machtfülle und Reichtum avanciert, so daß ihm 1489 kurzerhand der Kopf abgeschlagen wurde – um ihn dann Jahrhunderte später reumütig mit dem bescheidenen Denkmal doch noch zu ehren. Obwohl Zürich im 19. Jahrhundert zum unangefochtenen Wirtschaftszentrum der Schweiz geworden ist, tut man sich heute noch schwer im Umgang mit Größe und übt sich eher in zwinglianischer Freudlosigkeit und Bescheidenheit. Diese Haltung hat ihren Niederschlag auch in der Stadtbaugeschichte gefunden. Trotz erheblichen Reichtums vieler Zürcher Bürger ist die Stadt vergleichbar arm an Villen mit großen Gärten geblieben.

Um die Mitte des letzten Jahrhunderts setzte eine rege Bautätigkeit ein, in der neben zahlreichen kleinen auch einige größere Villen und Parkanlagen wie das Belvoirgut, die Villa Wesendonck oder Seeburg gebaut wurden. Die Gärten und Parkanlagen wurden beinahe ausnahmslos im spätklassizistischen Landschaftsgartenstil angelegt, und dies offenbar ungeachtet der Größe der Grundstücke. Im Trend der Zeit lag auch die vielfältige Verwendung von exotischen Sträuchern und Bäumen und die Anlage buntfarbener Teppichbeete. Als typische Schweizer Eigenart wurden die ohnehin zu kleinen Ziergärten durch das Anlegen von Obst- und Gemüsegärten in ihrer Präsentation weiter verkleinert. Nur ja nicht zu großartig, zu üppig, zu weitläufig, sondern immer vermischt mit dem Nützlichen und Praktischen scheint das verbreitete Credo – nicht nur für die Zürcher Gärten – gewesen zu sein. In diese Charakteristik passen der Garten und die Villa Wehrli geradezu idealtypisch.

Zurich Stories
Garden Villa Wehrli in Zurich

Hans Waldmann's equestrian statue is placed – in a literal sense, somewhat casually – at the bridge corner of the Limmat river. Being reserved1 in an urban sense, with an outstanding modesty in its location and dimension, it reveals some characteristics of the city of Zwingli, the city of the guilds and of economy. Given his success in war and economy, the commander-in-chief, Waldmann, advanced quickly to being a Renaissance potentate of such (untypical) power and wealth that in 1489 he was decapitated without hesitation – only to be ruefully commemorated and honored a couple of centuries later with this modest monument. Although Zurich had become the undisputed economic center of Switzerland by the 19th century, the inhabitants still have problems dealing with greatness and, therefore, would rather practice the Zwinglian penchant for unhappiness and modesty. This attitude has also been reflected in the urban architectural history. Despite the considerable wealth of many of Zurich's citizens, the city itself has remained rather poor with respect to villas with large gardens.

Around the middle of the past century, an active construction phase set in during which, aside from the many small villas being created, some larger estates and a num-

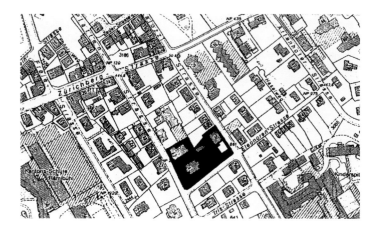

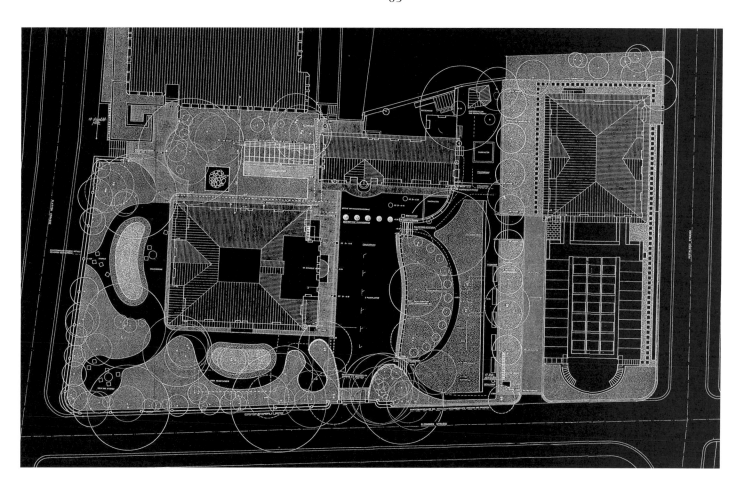

1868–71 ließ die gerade 40 Jahre alt gewordene, wohlhabende Witwe Juditha Wehrli-Nägeli Villa, Ökonomiegebäude und (vermutlich auch den) Garten durch Architekt Johann Caspar Ulrich d. J. an der Plattenstraße erstellen. Das Grundstück war zunächst 3500 m² groß, angesichts der Lage und des Reichtums der Besitzerin ein eher kleines Anwesen. Die Villa, symmetrisch konzipiert mit einem kräftigen Mittelrisalit, orientiert sich zur Pestalozzistraße und hat auf drei Seiten jeweils 10–12 Meter tief Gartenland aufzuweisen. Abgehoben vom Straßenniveau, die Hanglage ausnützend, thront sie, eingeengt im zu kleinen Grundstück, über der Straßenmauer und profitiert noch 40 Jahre lang vom freien Blick über das leere Grundstück auf der anderen Straßenseite.

ber of parks were being laid out, such as the Belvoirgut, Wesendonck Villa or Seeburg. The gardens and parks, almost without exception, were laid out in the late classicist landscape garden style despite the size of the properties. It was the trend of the times to use exotic shrubs and trees and to lay out colorful carpet beds. As a typical Swiss characteristic the much-too-small ornamental gardens were made even smaller in their presentation by laying out fruit and vegetable gardens. The credo seems to have been – and not only for the gardens of Zurich – to take care not to get too great, too full, too expansive, but instead to keep mixing in the useful and practical. The Wehrli Villa and the garden match these characteristics almost in a perfectly typical way.

Projektplan 1989
Grundriß
Original 1:100, 69 x 126 cm;
Lichtpause invertiert

Project plan 1989
Ground plan
Original 1:100, 69 x 126 cm;
blueprint inverted

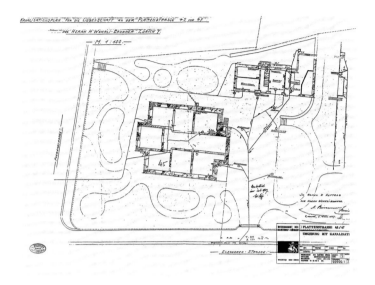

Von der Gartenanlage sind wenig Unterlagen vorhanden. Pläne und Bestand zeigen auf der Süd- und Westseite sich etwas gequält windende Wege, die zu zwei Sitzplätzen führen, und zwei axial angeordnete Teppichbeete. Auf kleinstem Raum wurden eine Fülle verschiedener, immergrüner Bäume und symmetrisch zum Gebäude zwei Platanen gepflanzt. Der Gartenteil zur Plattenstraße zeigt auch heute noch alte Obstbäume, einen geschwungenen Weg und ein altes, gußeisernes Spielgerät. Dies läßt vermuten, daß dieser größte Gartenbereich als Spielwiese, Obst- und Gemüsegarten der Nützlichkeit verpflichtet war. Nach der Jahrhundertwende wurde entlang der Plattenstraße eine weitere Villa gebaut und so der Garten um 1000 m² kleiner. Mit dem Erwerb durch die Universität 1966 zieht Geschäftigkeit in Haus und Garten ein. Das Ökonomiegebäude wird von Architekt P. Bolliger zu einem Tageshort umgebaut, anschließend erhält die Villa an der Pestalozzistraße durch M. Kaspar einen expressiven Bibliotheksanbau.

Der Garten stellt die Verbindung zwischen den drei unterschiedlich genutzten Gebäuden her. Im Nahbereich der Villa Wehrli ist die historische Substanz – Wege und Einfassungen, Bäume und Sträucher – größtenteils noch vorhanden, so daß sich die Eingriffe hauptsächlich auf Instandsetzungsarbeiten beschränkten. Einiges Kopfzer-

From 1868 to 1871, the 40 year old affluent widow, Juditha Wehrli-Nägeli, had the architect, Johann Caspar Ulrich (the younger), erect the villa, the economic buildings and, probably, the garden at Plattenstrasse. At first, the property had a size of 3500 square meters which was, given the location and the wealth of the proprietor, a rather small estate. The villa, which is conceived symmetrically with a strong central projection, orients itself towards Pestalozzistrasse and is surrounded on three sides by 10 to 12 meters of garden land. Elevated from the street level and using the slope, it sits throne-like above the street wall, restricted by the much-too-small property and, for 40 years, enjoying the view of the empty property across the street.

Only a few documents of the garden layout still exist today. The plans and the population on the south and west sides show somewhat tortured winding pathways leading to two sitting areas and two axially arranged carpet beds. In the smallest space, a wealth of different evergreen trees were planted and, placed symmetrically to the building, there are two sycamores. The part of the garden facing Plattenstrasse still reveals old fruit trees, a winding pathway, and old, cast-iron playground equipment. This leads to the assumption that this area, the largest part of the garden, was dedicated to usefulness as a playground, an orchard, and a vegetable garden. After the turn of the century, another villa was built along Plattenstrasse and the garden lost about 1000 square meters. After the university bought the property in 1966, life and activity moved into the house and garden. The commercial building was converted by the architect, P. Bolliger, into a day-care center. After that, the villa obtained an expressive library-addition at Pestalozzistrasse.

The garden represents the connection between the three buildings and their different use. In the close vicinity of the Wehrli Villa, the historic substance – pathways and frames, trees and shrubs – have been preserved for the most part causing the changes to be limited mainly to renovation work. The handling of the trees and shrubs caused some headaches. As mentioned before, the first plantings were much too densely set and the villa almost suffocates

Kanalisationsplan 1927
Grundriß
Original 1:100, 58 x 82 cm

Sewer system plan 1927
Ground plan
Original 1:100, 58 x 82 cm

brechen bereitete der Umgang mit Bäumen und Sträuchern. Wie bereits oben erwähnt, wurde schon bei der Erstbepflanzung viel zu dicht gepflanzt, so daß die Villa heute im Baumbestand beinahe erstickt. Das Prinzip der malerisch angeordneten, vielfältigen Koniferenpflanzung wird fortgeschrieben, wobei die Anzahl – insbesondere bei den Fichten – deutlich reduziert wurde. Die symmetrischen Platanen zur Plattenstraße werden wieder unter Schnitt gehalten. Stauden- und Wechselflorpflanzungen variieren die Randpartien des Gartens. Die alten Sitzplätze und der in der Mitte gelegene Aussichtsplatz eignen sich bestens für die neue Nutzung, selbst wenn – oder gerade weil – sich die Aussicht zur Straße und zu den Nachbargärten erschöpft.

Die Obstwiese wird zur Spielwiese des Kinderhortes. So finden die neu gepflanzten Beerensträucher und Obstbäume ihren direkten Abnehmer. Und auch das alte Spielgerät erweist sich nach seiner Instandstellung als mindestens so geeignet wie das vorhandene, spielpädagogisch hervorragende, druckimprägnierte Holzgerät. Der Bibliotheksneubau bildet den erhöhten Gartenabschluß. Ihm vorgelagert sind parallele Schichten von Hecken, Bankreihe, Mauer, Baumreihe und Erschließungsweg. Diese Schichten sind Teil des Neubaues und vermitteln gleichzeitig zum alten Garten.

Abschließend kann festgestellt werden: die Gebäude sind zurückhaltend saniert, die neue, öffentliche Nutzung ist ausgezeichnet und das kostbare Anwesen bestmöglich verwendet, ohne den Garten zu überbauen. Dieser ist sorgfältig instandgesetzt und auf den neuen Gebrauch ausgerichtet. Das Neue steht dem Alten klar ablesbar gegenüber, und auch der wichtige Unterhalt wird jetzt kontinuierlich und mit viel Sachverstand durchgeführt.

Wie eingangs angeführt, ist die Villa Wehrli mit ihrer Geschichte geradezu idealtypisch für die zürcherischen Charaktereigenschaften. Doch darf nicht unbeachtet bleiben, daß neben den etwas biederen Zürcher Eigenschaften eine Qualität doch vergessen wurde: Wie wäre es sonst zu erklären, daß in der gutbürgerlichen Villa Wehrli die Marxistin Rosa Luxemburg von 1894–95 Gastrecht genossen hat.

Erika Kienast-Lüder

beneath the tree population. The principle of the painterly arrangement of multiple conifers is continued, while the number – especially of the fir trees – was clearly reduced. The symmetrically placed sycamores towards Plattenstrasse are again trimmed into shape. Shrubs and changing floral plants vary the border parts of the garden. The old sitting areas and the lookout in the middle are perfectly suitable for the new function even if – or maybe because – the view is limited to the street and the neighboring gardens.

The orchard becomes the playground for the day-care-center. Thus, the newly planted berry bushes and fruit trees find a direct purpose and use. And the old playground equipment, after its renovation, proves to be just as fit as the new pressure-treated wooden ones, which are excellent in a pedagogical sense. The new library building forms the elevated garden termination. In front of it are parallel layers of hedges, a row of benches, the wall, rows of trees, and the access pathway. These layers are part of the new building and at the same time mediate towards the old garden.

In the end we can conclude that the buildings were renovated in a reserved way. The new public utilization is excellent, and the precious property is used in the best way possible without building over the garden. The garden has been carefully made over and directed towards the new utilization. The new can be clearly differentiated from the old and the important maintenance work is now done continually and with great expertise.

As mentioned in the beginning, the Wehrli Villa with its history is an ideally typical example of the Zurich characteristics. However, we should not neglect the fact that, aside from the somewhat honorable Zurich characteristics, one quality was overlooked. How else could we explain that the Marxist Rosa Luxemburg enjoyed the hospitality in the honorable Wehrli Villa from 1894 to 1895.

Erika Kienast-Lüder

Der Gartenteil zur Plattenstraße zeigt auch heute noch alte Obstbäume, einen geschwungenen Weg und ein altes, gußeisernes Spielgerät.

The part of the garden facing Plattenstrasse still reveals old fruit trees, a winding pathway, and old, cast-iron playground equipment.

Der Bibliotheksneubau bildet den erhöhten Gartenabschluß. Ihm vorgelagert sind parallele Schichten von Hecken, Bankreihe, Mauer, Baumreihe und Erschließungsweg. Diese Schichten sind Teil des Neubaues und vermitteln gleichzeitig zum alten Garten.

The new library building forms the elevated garden termination. In front of it are parallel layers of hedges, a row of benches, the wall, rows of trees, and the access pathway. These layers are part of the new building and at the same time mediate towards the old garden.

Die alten Sitzplätze und der in der Mitte gelegene Aussichtsplatz
eignen sich bestens für die neue Nutzung, selbst wenn – oder gerade weil
– sich die Aussicht zur Straße und zu den Nachbargärten erschöpft.

The old sitting areas and the lookout in the middle are perfectly suitable
for the new function even if – or maybe because – the view is limited to the street
and the neighboring gardens.

Illusion und Wirklichkeit

Wenn Walser meint, daß die schönsten Gärten die erdachten oder beschriebenen Gärten seien, hat er sicher soweit recht, als er den Garten als etwas Vollkommenes, durch keinerlei Störungen beeinflußtes Ganzes versteht. Seit der Vertreibung aus dem Paradies wissen wir aber, daß der Garten eben nicht mehr Paradies, sondern nur noch dessen Sehnsuchtsraum darstellt. Unsere heutigen Gärten reiben sich an den alltäglichen Einflüssen und Störungen von Innen und Außen. Und häufig wird erst in der Differenz zum Umfeld die relativ «heile Welt» des Gartens manifest. Die Wirklichkeiten sind große und kleine Störungen, in deren Intensität der Wechsel zur Belästigung deutlich wird: Die verstellte Aussicht, das allzu kleine Grundstück, die schlechte Architektur, das Gebell des Nachbarhundes oder die Geschwätzigkeit des Postboten.

Der erfinderische Umgang mit den vorgegebenen Rahmenbedingungen ist selbstverständlicher Teil unserer Gartengestaltungen, die zwischen einem kritischen und illusionserzeugenden Ansatz oszillieren. Unter Illusion ist dabei weniger die Verweigerung der Wirklichkeit gemeint, sondern vielmehr die Steigerung der Wahrnehmung und Erfahrbarkeit. So kann der Garten zum Kompendium vielschichtiger Bedeutungsebenen werden, in denen Illusion und Wirklichkeit kaleidoskopartig miteinander verbunden sind. Auf diesem heiklen Gang begleiten uns unsere Bauherrschaften, denen häufig die ungestörte Illusion ein zentrales Anliegen ist. In gemeinsamen Gesprächen entwickeln wir dann eine Lesart der Situation, die sich an den Qualitäten und weniger an den Mängeln des Ortes orientiert.

Die ehemalige Ausbildung des Garten S. bricht sich in vielen Teilen an störenden Wirklichkeiten: die Landschaftsgartenkonzeption an zu geringer Raumtiefe, die Aussicht an falsch plazierten Tannen, der Wasserspiegel des Swimmingpools an der hellblauen Farbe und die Erfahrbarkeit des gesamten Gartens am schlecht gelegenen Sitzplatz direkt am Haus.

Illusion and Reality

If Walser says that the most beautiful gardens are those thought out or described, he is certainly right as far as he understands the garden as something perfect, undisturbed and uninfluenced – the garden as a whole. However, since the expulsion from paradise we know that the garden is no longer paradise. But it represents its own space of desire. Today's gardens are confronted with the every-day influences and disturbances from within and without. And very often the relatively 'whole world' of the garden becomes manifest only through the difference with the environment. The realities are big and small disturbances; in their intensity, the shift towards annoyance becomes clear: the blocked view, the much-too-small plot, the bad architecture, the barking of the neighbor's dog or the gossip of the postman.

The inventive handling of the existing frame conditions is a self-understood part of our garden designs, which oscillate between a critical and illusory approach. The illusion in this case is not so much the refusal of reality, but more the increase of our perception and ability to experience. Thus, the garden can become a compendium of multi-layered levels of meaning where illusion and reality are connected with each other in a kaleidoscopic way. We

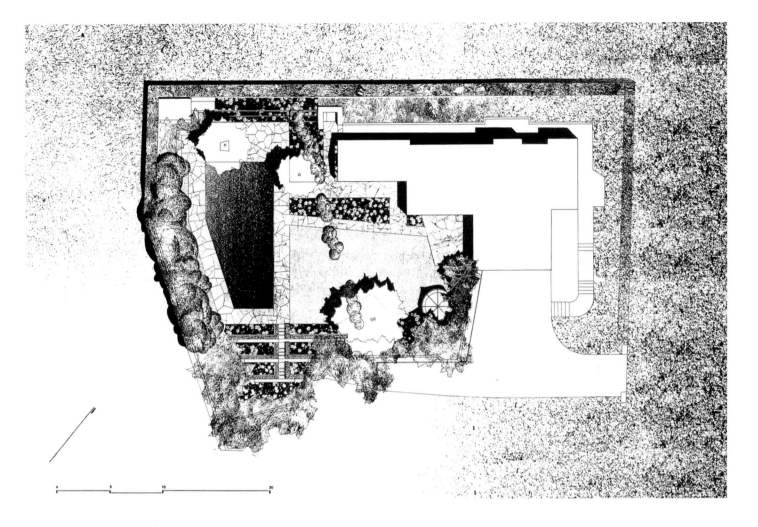

Die Entwicklung einer differenzierten Raumstruktur war wegleitend für die Umgestaltung des Gartens. Unterschiedliche Raumtiefen werden durch Pflanzenschichten angestrebt. Die kleine Rasenfläche wird durch eine frei geschnittene Buchshecke scheinbar zweigeteilt, ein großer Japanischer Ahorn und eine Magnolie stoßen in den Hauptraum vor. Durch die neu gefaßten Aussichtsfenster wird der Blick in die offene Umgebung und Voralpen inszeniert, während die direkt angrenzenden Gebäude nur mehr von der talseitigen Hangkante aus sichtbar sind. Die «geborgte Landschaft» außerhalb des Gartens wird zur letzten Schicht einer gestaffelten Raumfolge, die gerade

are accompanied on this tricky walk by our clients, whose central cause is often the undisturbed illusion. In discussions, we develop a way of reading the situation which is oriented more towards the qualities than to the deficiencies of the location.

The former layout of the garden S. breaks down in many areas due to the disturbing realities of the situation: the conception of the landscape garden due to the low spatial depth, the view due to wrongly placed pine trees, the water mirror of the pool due to the light blue color, the ability to experience the entire garden due to the badly placed sitting area directly by the house.

Projektplan 1990 (96)
Grundriß
Original 1:100, 45 x 70 cm;
Tusche, Farbstift,
Folie auf Plandruck weiß

Project plan 1990 (96),
Ground plan
Original 1:100, 45 x 70 cm;
ink, colored pencil,
foil on white plan print

durch die Einengung Weite erzielt. Der neu mit dunklem Naturstein ausgelegte Pool hat seine eindeutige Nutzung verloren und ist zum Spiegel der unregelmäßig geschnittenen, fünf Meter hohen Eibenwand geworden. Die Kanten der vorhandenen, polygonal verlegten Granitplatten wurden geometrisiert, ein neuer Weg führt zum Wasserbecken und zum dahinterliegenden Sitzplatz, der eine bisher nicht gekannte Raumwahrnehmung des Gartens offeriert.

Anstelle der üblichen Polyantharosenbeete wurden differenzierte Staudenrabatten mit eingestreuten Parkrosen bepflanzt, deren enges Farbenspektrum sich zwischen weiß und pink bewegt. Unterhalb der Hangkante verbergen sich kleine Stufenterrassen, auf denen die Schnittstauden angepflanzt sind.

Material- und Pflanzenverwendung, Raumsequenzen und sinnliche Wahrnehmung verdeutlichen, daß hier ein neuer Garten entstanden ist, der gleichzeitig auch alter Garten geblieben ist. Die Illusion ist zur Wirklichkeit, die Wirklichkeit zur Illusion geworden.

Dieter Kienast

The development of a differentiated spatial structure was guiding our way to the redesign of the garden. Different spatial depths are striven for with layers of plants. The small lawn is seemingly divided into two parts by a box hedge, a large Japanese maple tree and a magnolia tree projecting into the main space. The vista of the open environment and the foothills of the Alps is produced through the newly framed view windows, while the directly adjoining buildings can be seen only from the edge of the slope facing the valley. The "borrowed landscape" outside of the garden becomes the last layer of a stepped sequence of spaces which attains width just because of the restriction. The pool which has received new, dark, natural stone tiles has lost its clear utilization and has become the mirror of the irregularly cut five meter high wall of yew trees. The edges of the existing granite tiles were made more geometric; a new pathway leads to the water basin and the sitting area behind it which now offers a formerly unknown spatial perception of the garden.

Instead of the usual polyantha rose beds, various narrow beds with shrubs interspersed with park roses were planted. Their narrow color spectrum goes from white to pink. Below the edge of the slope, small stepped terraces are cut into the incline and planted with trimmed shrubs.

The use of materials and plants, spatial sequences and sensual perception make clear that a new garden was created here which, at the same time, has remained the old garden. The illusion has become reality, reality has become illusion.

Dieter Kienast

Unterhalb der Hangkante verbergen sich kleine Stufenterrassen, auf denen die Schnittstauden angepflanzt sind.

Below the edge of the slope, small stepped terraces are cut into the incline and planted with trimmed shrubs.

Unterschiedliche Raumtiefen werden durch Pflanzenschichten angestrebt.
Die kleine Rasenfläche wird durch eine frei geschnittene Buchshecke scheinbar
zweigeteilt, ein großer Japanischer Ahorn ...

Different spatial depths are striven for with layers of plants. The small lawn is seemingly divided into two parts by a box hedge, a large Japanese maple tree ...

Wo ist Arkadien?

Gärten zu bauen heißt Geschichten erleben. Geschichten mögen ein Ende haben, während Gärten nie fertig werden. So haben auch unsere Gartengeschichten – die guten wenigstens – kein Ende, sondern es werden ihnen neue Kapitel hinzugefügt. Diese Geschichte beginnt 1989. Das ältere Ehepaar E. besitzt am Üetliberg ein riesiges Grundstück. Darauf steht ein einfaches Haus aus den Fünfzigerjahren mit einem belanglosen Garten, der nur einen kleinen Teil des Grundstückes beansprucht. Ein zweiter Teil wird als Weide genutzt, ein dritter Teil besteht aus einem 50 Meter steil abfallenden, alten Buchenwald. Die Aussicht ist gegen Westen beeindruckend weit über sanft gewellte Hügel bis zu den Alpen.

Die Kinder von Frau und Herrn E. sind längst «ausgeflogen», ihr Geschäft haben sie verkauft. Den Garten pflegen sie mit Umsicht, sind aber etwas unzufrieden, weil die angepflanzten Sträucher die Aussicht versperren. Sie geben uns den Auftrag, ihren Garten neu zu planen. Auch nach längerem Gespräch wird lediglich der Wunsch nach einem Stauden- und Kräuterbeet deutlich. Ansonsten wünschen sie sich einen schöneren Garten. Wir bleiben im Ungewissen, wieviel Umgestaltung aus ihrer Sicht möglich und notwendig ist.

Der Befund vor Ort führt uns zu folgenden Schlüssen: Der enge, sichtverhindernde Strauchgürtel muß entfernt, die steile Böschung abgeflacht und die markante Baumkulisse ins Blickfeld gerückt werden. Sie bildet zugleich die natürliche Grenze des kultivierten Gartens gegen Süden. An der Westgrenze steht eine hundert Meter lange Weißdornhecke, die allzu hoch aufgewachsen ist und dadurch die Aussicht vom Gebäude in die Hügel- und Alpenlandschaft versperrt, während sie von der unteren Gartenebene als Raumgrenze hohe Qualität aufweist. Eine schöne Obstbaumwiese steigt sanft zum Üetliberg an, ist allerdings von Haus und Garten isoliert. Der Waldrand markiert zugleich die obere Hangkante und würde einen beeindruckenden Blick in das 50 Meter tiefer liegende Bachtobel (das eben-

Where is Arcadia?

Designing gardens means experiencing stories. Stories may have an end while gardens are never completed. In this sense, our garden stories – at least the good ones – don't have an end, but new chapters are always being added to them. This story begins in 1989. The elderly couple E. owns a huge property at Uetliberg. On it stands a simple house dating back to the fifties with an unimportant garden which takes up only a small part of the property. A second part is used as a pasture and a third consists of an old beech forest sloping steeply down about 50 meters. The view towards the west is impressively broad and reaches from soft foothills up to the Alps.

The children of Mrs. and Mr. E. have long 'left the nest' and they have sold their business. They carefully tend their garden, but they are somewhat unhappy because the planted shrubs block the view. They have asked us to redesign their garden. Even after a longer conversation, only the wish for a shrub and herb bed becomes clear. Otherwise, they wish only for a more beautiful garden. We are left with the uncertainty about how much of a redesign is possible and necessary in their view.

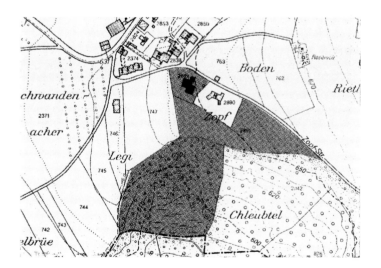

falls noch zum Grundstück gehört) bieten, wenn nicht dichtes Brombeergebüsch die Einsicht verhindern würde.

Unser erstes Projekt von 1989 konzentriert die Interventionen zwischen Gebäude und Waldrand. Die Topographie wird, dem früheren Gelände entsprechend, sanft abfallend planiert. Das Gebäude steht virtuell auf einem Betonplattenbelag mit weit gezogenen Fugen, in denen Mentha und Thymian eingesät werden. Die flankierende Eibenhecke bietet Windschutz und Rahmen für die vorgelagerte Staudenrabatte. Vom Sitzplatz und Gebäude aus wird der Blick durch Hecke und Eibenkegel auf den Waldrand und einen Teil des schmalen Wasserbeckens gelenkt. Die Buchstreppen hinuntergehend, wird das ganze Becken in seiner sich scheinbar verändernden Form sichtbar. Die Weißdornhecke ist neu beschnitten, unter den überhängenden Zweigen entdecken wir einen Treillagengang. Am Wasser sitzend, wird der Blick auf den vorher verborgenen Gartenteil der Obstbaumwiese frei. Der Waldrand und damit auch die Hangkante werden durch eine geschnittene Feldahornhecke präzisiert. Eine natürlich vorhandene Kanzel wird zum Aussichtspunkt gestaltet. Der Blick fällt hinunter, auf die im Hang entspringende Quelle, den Bach und das tief unten liegende Waldplateau oder auf die darüber ansetzende Lichtung zum Üetliberg. Der Aussichtspunkt wird zum bedeutungsvollsten Ort des Gartens, zu einem altbekannten Topos: dem inszenierten Aufeinanderprallen der lieblich gezähmten Natur des Gartens mit der wilden Natur des steil abfallenden Waldhanges. Ein Geländer, als Schriftzug ausgebildet, schützt vor dem Hinunterfallen und wird selber zum Gartenblickpunkt.

Schriften im Garten sind in der Gartengeschichte altbekannt. Erinnert sei an Orsinis «Heiligen Wald von Bomarzo», an die Inschriften in Englischen Landschaftsgärten wie Stowe, Wörlitz oder Ermenonville. In den letzten Jahren beobachten wir eine Wiederentdeckung der Schriften, selbstverständlich in der Werbung, aber auch in der Architektur und vor allem in der Kunst. Aus der bildenden Kunst nennen wir stellvertretend die Arbeiten von Jenny Holzer und Fischli/Weiss. Ian Hamilton Finlay hat den Brückenschlag zwischen Literatur und Gartenkunst erneut vollzogen und in vielen Gärten aufsehenerregende Arbeiten ge-

The on-site diagnosis leads us to the following conclusions: the narrow view-blocking belt of shrubbery must be removed, the steep slop needs to be flattened out and the striking tree scenery must be put into the center of perception. It also forms the natural border of the cultivated garden towards the south. On the western border, a one hundred meter long hawthorn hedge which has grown too high blocks the view from the building towards the landscape of the foothills and Alps; however, seen from the lower garden level, it has a high quality as a spatial border. A beautiful orchard softly raises up towards Uetliberg but is isolated from the house and the garden. The edge of the

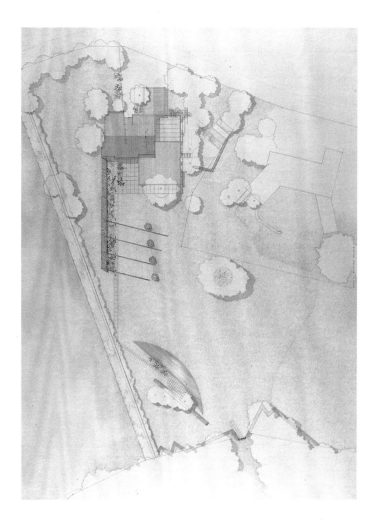

Projektplan 1. Phase 1989
Grundriß
Original 1:100, 87 x 118 cm;
Bleistift und Farbstift
auf grauem Halbkarton

Project plan 1st phase 1989
Ground plan
Original 1:100, 87 x 118 cm;
pencil and colored pencil
on gray semi-cardboard

schaffen. Die Gemeinsamkeit aller Schriftinstallationen ist der wechselnde Bedeutungsgehalt ihrer Rezeption.

Auch uns hat die ambivalente Lesart des Schriftzuges interessiert. «Differentia» war unser erster Vorschlag, womit wir auf die unterschiedlichen Naturformen von Garten und Wildnis, den versteckten Höhensprung oder den Wechsel von der früheren zur neuen Gartengestaltung gezielt haben.

Zu unserer Überraschung fand unser Projekt ungeteilte Zustimmung, mit der einzigen Ausnahme: die Wahl des «Brüstungswortes». Der Garten wurde gebaut und von den Besitzern nicht nur liebevoll in Pflege genommen. Vielmehr ist der Garten zu ihrer sinnstiftenden Lebensarbeit geworden. Auf unzähligen Gartenrundgängen haben wir über mögliche und notwendige Pflege- und Gestaltungsarbeiten gesprochen. Literatur wurde gewälzt, auf vielen Exkursionen im In- und Ausland neue Eindrücke gesammelt, Pflanzen mitgebracht und eingepflanzt. Und immer wieder neue Schriftzüge wurden erwogen, bis unser letzter Vorschlag «Et in Arcadia ego» ihre ungeteilte Zustimmung fand.

Arkadien, von Vergil erstmals beschrieben, ist weniger die reale Landschaft in Griechenland, sondern geistige Landschaft, die Metapher der glückseligen, naturverbun-

forest also marks the upper edge of the slope and would offer an impressive view into the ravine 50 meters lower down (which also belongs to the property), if it were not prevented by dense blackberry shrubs.

Our first project in 1989 concentrated the interventions between the building and the edge of the forest. The topography is planed down to be softly sloping, according to the former grounds. The building is situated on a concrete tile surface with wide seams in which mint and thyme are sowed. The adjoining yew hedge provides protection from the wind and the frame for the narrow shrub bed in the front. The vista from the sitting area and the building is guided through the hedge and the yew cone towards the edge of the forest and a part of the narrow water basin. When descending the box steps, the entire basin with its seemingly changing form becomes visible. The hawthorn hedge is trimmed back and beneath the overhanging branches we discover a covered walk. Sitting by the water, the view of the once hidden part of the garden with the orchard is now free. The edge of the forest, and thus the slope, is made more precise by a trimmed field maple hedge. A naturally existing pulpit is designed as a lookout point. The view descends to the spring with its source in the slope, to the brook and the forest plateau far below, or to the clearing towards Uetliberg starting above. The lookout becomes the most important place in the garden, a well-known topos: the produced collision of the rather tamed nature of the garden with the wild nature of the steeply sloping forest hill. A balustrade in the form of an inscription provides protection from falling off and becomes a center of interest in itself.

Inscriptions in the gardens have been well-known throughout their history. We recall Orsini's 'Holy Forest of Bomarzo' and the inscriptions in English landscape gardens such as Stowe, Wörlitz or Ermenonville. In recent years, we have observed a rediscovery of the script – certainly in advertising, but also in architecture and, above all, in art. For the latter, we name representatively the works by Jenny Holzer and Fischli/Weiss. Ian Hamilton Finlay has again built the bridge between literature and the art of gardening and has created works in many gardens which

Nicolas Poussin
«Et in Arcadia ego»
(ca. 1638/39, 2. Fassung)
Musée du Louvre, Paris

Nicolas Poussin
"Et in Arcadia ego"
(approx. 1638/39, 2nd version),
Musée du Louvre, Paris

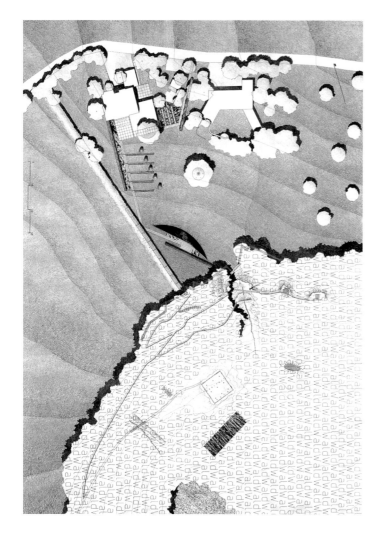

denen Hirtenidylle. Bekannt geworden ist die Inschrift erstmals auf einem Bild Guercinos (ca. 1621/23): zwei Hirten bei der Betrachtung einer Grabstätte mit einer Inschrift und einem großen Totenschädel. «Et in Arcadia ego» heißt nach Panofsky richtig übersetzt: «Auch ich bin da, ich existiere, sogar in Arkadien.» Gemeint ist der Tod, der auch im glücklichen Land Arkadien gegenwärtig ist. Populär geworden ist das Motiv durch zwei Bilder Poussins (ca. 1630 und 1639 gemalt). Lévi-Strauss zeigt in seiner scharfsinnigen Analyse, wie die Verbindung zum Tod bei Poussin abnimmt und der Totenschädel im zweiten Bild fehlt (vgl. Ab-

gain a lot of notoriety. What all script installations have in common is the changing meaning of their content in their reception.

We too were interested in the ambivalent way of reading the inscription. "Differentia" was our first proposal and with it we took aim at the different natural forms of garden and wilderness, the hidden change in altitude or the change from the former to the new garden design.

To our surprise, our project was met with undivided consent with only one exception: the choice of the 'balustrade word'. The garden was converted and taken over by the proprietors not only for care-taking, but also and perhaps more importantly, the garden has brought sense and meaning to their existence and has become their life's work.

On numerous garden tours we have discussed possible and necessary care and design work. We've pored over the literature and, on our many excursions both at home and abroad, have collected new impressions and brought back many plants and planted them. And ever new inscriptions were thought of, until finally our last proposal "Et in Arcadia ego" found the proprietor's complete approval.

Arcadia, once described by Virgil, is not so much the real landscape of Greece, but the spiritual landscape, the metaphor of the blissful shepherd's ideal close to nature. The inscription first became famous from a painting by Guercino (ca. 1621/23). It depicts two shepherds looking at a grave with an inscription and a large skull. According to Panofsky, "Et in Arcadia ego" means : 'I too am there, I exist, even in Arcadia'. What is meant is death, which is also present in the happy land of Arcadia. The motif has become popular only by two paintings by Poussin which he painted in ca.1630 and ca.1639. Lévi-Strauss shows in his sharp analysis how the relation with death gets lost in Poussin's paintings and the skull is missing in the second painting (see picture). In the 18th century, the inscription was finally completely detached from the grave scene and received a new meaning with various authors, such as Herder, Schiller and Goethe: 'I too have enjoyed bliss', or 'I too have lived in the blissful peaceful shepherd's land of Arcadia'.

Projektplan, Gesamtplan
2. Phase 1994
Original 1:200, 70 x 100 cm;
Tusche, Farbstift
auf Plandruck weiß

Project plan, entire plan
2nd phase 1994
Original 1:200, 70 x 100 cm;
ink, colored pencil
on white plan print

bildung). Im 18. Jahrhundert erfährt der Schriftzug seine endgültige Loslösung von der Grabstätte und erhält jetzt bei Autoren wie Herder, Schiller und Goethe eine geänderte Bedeutung: «Auch ich habe das Glück genossen» oder «Auch ich habe im glücklichen, friedfertigen Hirtenland Arkadien gelebt.»

In unserem Garten am Üetliberg wird der Brüstungsschriftzug zum stärksten, narrativen Element, das eine Vielzahl an Assoziationen, Interpretationen und Deutungen zuläßt: Von der Landschaftsmalerei, den Dichtern, die sich mit Gärten befaßt haben, bis hin zur Lebensgeschichte des Besitzerpaares.

«Et in Arcadia ego» wird zum Ausgangspunkt und Generator der zweiten Bauetappe von 1994, in der der dramatische Waldhang ‹entdeckt› wird – nicht von uns, sondern zunächst von Herrn E., der einen gefährlich steilen Weg, Treppen und eine Brücke anlegt. Auch hier wird unbewußt einem klassischen Verhaltensmuster gefolgt: Nachdem der Garten ausreichend kultiviert worden ist, erfolgen die Ein- und Übergriffe in die Wildnis. Unsere geplanten Interventionen zielen nicht auf eine Gartenerweiterung, sondern beschränken sich auf wenige Eingriffe, mittels derer die wilde Natur besser erlebt werden kann. Wichtigstes Element ist ein intensiv blau eingefärbter Handlauf, der wegbegleitend ein einigermaßen sicheres Hinuntersteigen erlaubt. Zwei kleine Sitzplätze an markanten Orten und einige wenige, auf die vorhandene Waldvegetation abgestimmte Pflanzungen weisen auf die sanfte Inanspruchnahme der wilden Natur.

Wir sitzen auf der Waldbank und erinnern uns – Arkadien ist an einem anderen Ort.

Dieter Kienast

In our garden at Uetliberg, the balustrade inscription becomes the strongest narrative element, allowing for a multitude of associations and interpretations: from the landscape painters, to the poets dealing with gardens, to the life story of the proprietors.

"Et in Arcadia ego" becomes the starting point and impetus for the second construction phase in 1994 during which the dramatic forest slope is 'discovered' – not by us, but first by Mr. E., who laid out a dangerously steep pathway, steps, and a bridge. Unconsciously, a classical pattern of behavior is followed here, as well: after the garden has been sufficiently cultivated, the operations and infringements of the wilderness begin. Our planned interventions do not aim at an extension of the garden, but are limited to only a few operations through which the wild nature can be better experienced. The most important element is an intensively blue balustrade which accompanies a somewhat safer descent. Two small sitting areas in important places and a few plantings in harmony with the existing forest vegetation point to the gentle use of the wild nature.

We are sitting on the bench in the forest and remember – Arcadia is in a different place.

Dieter Kienast

Der Aussichtspunkt wird zum bedeutungsvollsten Ort des Gartens, zu einem altbekannten Topos: dem inszenierten Aufeinanderprallen der lieblich gezähmten Natur des Gartens mit der wilden Natur des steil abfallenden Waldhanges.

The lookout becomes the most important place in the garden, a well-known topos: the produced collision of the rather tamed nature of the garden with the wild nature of the steeply sloping forest hill.

Die Buchstreppen hinuntergehend, wird das ganze Becken
in seiner sich scheinbar verändernden Form sichtbar.

When descending the box steps, the entire basin with its seemingly changing form becomes visible.

In unserem Garten am Üetliberg wird der Brüstungsschriftzug zum stärksten, narrativen Element, das eine Vielzahl an Assoziationen, Interpretationen und Deutungen zuläßt: Von der Landschaftsmalerei, den Dichtern ...

In our garden at Uetliberg, the balustrade inscription becomes the strongest narrative element, allowing for a multitude of associations and interpretations: from the landscape painters, to the poets ...

... wenige Eingriffe, mittels derer die wilde Natur besser erlebt werden kann. Wichtigstes Element ist ein intensiv blau eingefärbter Handlauf, der wegbegleitend ein einigermaßen sicheres Hinuntersteigen erlaubt.

... few operations through which the wild nature can be better experienced. The most important element is an intensively blue balustrade which accompanies a somewhat safer descent.

Aussichten und Einsichten

Das Entwerfen von Gärten findet in der stillen Konzentration am Zeichentisch, aber auch in mehr oder weniger heftigen Gesprächen unter uns Partnern statt. Erst dabei wird deutlich, ob ein Konzept tragfähig genug ist, auch kritischen Einwänden standzuhalten. Besonders heftig wird die Diskussion, wenn die Pflanzungen besprochen werden. Diese wecken offensichtlich starke Emotionen, die einer vernunftbetonten Argumentation im Wege stehen. Dabei geht es weniger darum, einen Baum zu plazieren, eine Hecke oder Staudenrabatte zu setzen, vielmehr ist die Frage der Baumart, der Struktur der Hecke oder das Farben- und Formenspektrum der Staudenrabatte Gegenstand der Diskussion. Kaum erklärbare Vorlieben oder Abneigungen werden deutlich: Einer erachtet den malerischen Wuchs des Essigbaumes für zwingend, während der andere angewidert auf den pelzigen Fruchtstand und die penetrante Herbstfärbung verweist. Die Vorstellung einer frei geschnittenen Mischhecke steht derjenigen der geometrisch geschnittenen Buchshecke gegenüber.

Weil Annäherung oder Kompromiß meist ausgeschlossen sind, wirkt die Kraft des Faktischen – derjenige, der zeichnet, bestimmt. Erst auf gemeinsamen, späteren Gartenbegehungen wird Zustimmung oder Ablehnung der ausgeführten Pflanzung deutlich.

Übereinstimmung gibt es in der hohen Wertschätzung und Bedeutung, die wir unseren Pflanzungen beimessen. Pflanzen definieren den Gartenraum, tragen wesentlich zum Stimmungsgehalt des Gartens bei, sind Form und Farbe, Duft und Geräusch und stehen für die Alterungsfähigkeit des Gartens. Dabei schöpfen wir aus der ganzen Fülle – das Wildwachsende ebenso wie das sorgsam Kultivierte, das Einheimische und Fremde, der große Baum wie die kleine Moosritze.

Der Garten am Bodensee ist ein Beispiel unter vielen, welche Bedeutung Vegetation einnimmt, und wo ihre Grenzen erreicht werden. Das Grundstück liegt direkt am Bodensee, dessen flaches Ufer durch einen 50 Meter tiefen

Outlooks and Insights

The design of a garden happens through calm concentration at the drafting table and/or through more or less animated discussions between the partners. Only through this process can we become clear about whether a concept is thought through enough to withstand even the most critical arguments. The discussion gets especially lively when it comes to the plantings. This seems to evoke strong emotions which stand in the way of a reasonable argument. The point of concern is not the placing of a tree, a hedge or a bush bed; the center of discussion is rather the type of tree, the structure of the hedge or the color and form specter of the bush bed. Preference and dislikes which can hardly be explained become clear: one of us considers the painterly growth of the Rhus typhina (sumac) as a must, whereas another points out, almost with disgust, the furry fruits and the importunate fall foliage. The idea of a freely trimmed mixed hedge opposes that of the geometrically trimmed box hedge.

Because an approach or compromise is practically impossible, the force of the facts has its effect – the one who does the drafting makes the decision. Only during common walks through the garden at a later time can the consent or refusal for the realized plantings become clearer.

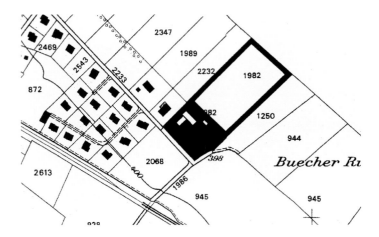

Schilfgürtel beeindruckend ausgezeichnet ist. Im Osten bildet ein Uferwald die dichte räumliche Grenze, entlang der Erschließungsstraße definieren einzelne alte Buchen den transparenten Übergang zum öffentlichen Bereich. Das Gebäude wurde in den 20er Jahren vom Bauhausschüler Schindler im Stil der klassischen Moderne als Badehaus konzipiert und zu Beginn der 90er Jahre als Wohnhaus für die Familie S. umgebaut. Der Garten lebte vom überwältigenden Blick aus dem Obergeschoß auf Schilfgürtel und See sowie das angrenzende Waldstück, das als Spielplatz für die Kinder hervorragende Qualität aufweist.

Zufahrt und Hauseingang werden durch geschnittene Buchen- und Spireenhecken gefaßt und damit wird gleichzeitig eine räumliche Grenze zum Uferweg geschaffen. Ein sonniger, windgeschützter Sitzplatz im Winkel der Hausform und ein Schattenplatz unter schirmförmig gezogenen Kastanien erweitern die Nutzung des Gartens. Bei unserer ersten Gartenbegehung haben wir auf den Rasen gefallene Buchenblätter bemerkt, die mit ihren Braun-

There is an agreement when it comes to the high valuation we attribute to our plantings. Plants define the garden space and contribute considerably to the atmospheric content of the garden. They are form and color, scent and sound, and they represent the ability of the garden to age. And we can refer to the whole wealth: the wildly growing as well as the carefully cultivated plants, the local and foreign, the large tree and the small gap filled with moss.

The garden at Lake Constance is one of many examples showing the importance the vegetation can have and where its limits are. The property is located directly at the lake whose flat shore is marked by a 50 meter deep belt of reed grass. To the east, a shoreline forest forms the dense spatial border, and along the access road some old beeches define the transparent transit to the public area. The house was built during the '20s by the Bauhaus-student, Schindler, in the classical modern style as a bath house and it was converted in the beginning of the '90s into a home for the S. family. The garden gained its life from the over-

Projektplan 1991 (96)
Grundriß
Original 1:100, 60 x 120 cm;
Tusche, Folie, Ölkreide
auf Großxerox weiß

Project plan 1991 (96)
Ground plan
Original 1:100, 60 x 120 cm;
ink, foil, oil crayon
on white Xerox copy

tönen das saftige grün des Rasens kontrastierten. In der Gestaltung der Staudenbeete wird das Thema aufgenommen. Die Buchenblätter wurden 50fach vergrößert, als Staudenbeete interpretiert und liegen richtungslos auf Platz und Rasen. Die ehemals unebene Rasenfläche wird in ihrer präzisierten Ausformung zur horizontalen Grundebene, über der – Höhenschichten gleich – Hecke, Schilf, Baumkrone und Himmel signifikant in Erscheinung treten. Das Thema der räumlichen Fassung war auch beim Eckplatz mit einem Stützenband geplant. Notwendig, um die unbestimmte Raumdefintion des Sitzplatzes zu klären. Ein Ersatz des Stützenbandes durch Vegetation erschien uns wegen des allzu starken architektonischen Bezuges zum Gebäude nicht möglich. Nachdem wir Familie S. von der Bedeutung der Stützen nicht überzeugen konnten, bleibt der Eckplatz räumlich ungeklärt und der inszenierte Kontrast zwischen der starren Stützengliederung und den «schwimmenden Staudenblättern» nur auf dem Plan und in unseren Köpfen ausformuliert.

Von der Gartenebene aus bleibt der Bodensee hinter dem hohen Schilfgürtel verborgen. Seine Präsenz wird durch den gedämpften Wellenschlag und den unverkennbaren Seegeruch manifest. Ein schmaler Weg und Holzsteg führt uns durch den Schilfgürtel zur offenen Wasserfläche. Zuvorderst auf der Stegbank erkennen wir landeinwärts das klein gewordene Haus mit seinen flankierenden Baumkronen, unter uns das klare Wasser und seewärts ausgedehnte Schilffelder und im leichten Dunst die Ahnung des weit entfernten, fremden Ufers.

Dieter Kienast

whelming vista from the upper floor to the belt of reeds and the lake and from the adjoining forest, which is excellent as a playground for the children.

The access and entrance to the house are framed by trimmed beech and Spiraea hedges; at the same time, this creates a spatial border to the shore path. A sunny sitting area, well protected from the wind in the corner of the house form and another in the shade beneath umbrella-like chestnut trees, expand the use of the garden. During our first walk through the garden, we noticed beech leaves on the lawn which formed a contrast to the rich green of the lawn itself. We have taken up this theme in the design of the bush beds. The beech leaves were enlarged 50 times, interpreted as bush beds and are placed without orientation on the square and the lawn. The formerly uneven lawn surface becomes the horizontal base plane in its precise design above which – similar to height levels – the hedge, reeds, tree crown and sky have a significant appearance. The theme of the spatial frame was planned with a belt of supports around the corner sitting area, as well. It was necessary to clarify its uncertain spatial definition. A replacement of the supports by vegetation seemed impossible to us due to the strong architectural reference to the building. As we have been unable to convince the S. family of the meaning of the supports, the corner square remains unclear in a spatial sense and the contrast between the stark arrangement of the supports and the 'floating bush leaves' was phrased in only on the plan and in our heads.

From the garden level, Lake Constance remains hidden beyond the high reeds. Its presence is manifested through the muffled sound of the waves and the unmistakable smell of the lake. A narrow pathway and wooden footbridge lead through the reeds to the open water surface. Sitting on the bench on the footbridge facing the land, we recognize the small silhouette of the house with the surrounding tree crowns; beneath us is the clear water and towards the lake are expansive fields of reeds. In the dim light of dusk we can just discern the remains of the distant and foreign shoreline.

Dieter Kienast

Die ehemals unebene Rasenfläche wird in ihrer präzisierten Ausformung zur horizontalen Grundebene, über der – Höhenschichten gleich – Hecke, Schilf, Baumkrone und Himmel signifikant in Erscheinung treten.

The formerly uneven lawn surface becomes the horizontal base plane in its precise design above which – similar to height levels – the hedge, reeds, tree crown and sky have a significant appearance.

... der Bodensee ... seine Präsenz wird durch den gedämpften Wellenschlag und den unverkennbaren Seegeruch manifest. Ein schmaler Weg und Holzsteg führt uns durch den Schilfgürtel zur offenen Wasserfläche.

... Lake Constance ... its presence is manifested through the muffled sound of the waves and the unmistakable smell of the lake. A narrow pathway and wooden footbridge lead through the reeds to the open water surface.

Ein sonniger, windgeschützter Sitzplatz im Winkel
der Hausform und ein Schattenplatz unter schirmförmig gezogenen
Kastanien erweitern die Nutzung des Gartens.

A sunny sitting area, well protected from the wind in the corner
of the house form and another in the shade beneath umbrella-like chestnut trees,
expand the use of the garden.

Ohne Kontext oder die Liebe zur Geometrie

Die Lage und Nachbarschaften eines Grundstückes sind wesentliche Rahmenbedingungen unserer Gartengestaltungen. In wenigen Fällen bleibt die Verweigerung des Kontextes als einzig sinnvoller Ausweg, so auch im vorliegenden Fall. Tatort ist ein neues Einfamilienhausquartier einer kleinen Gemeinde im Zürcher Oberland. Kennzeichnendes Merkmal des neuen Quartiers ist seine Merkmallosigkeit, die sich unauffällig in die Phalanx hunderter gleicher Einfamilienhausquartiere einordnet. Häuser und Gärten bestechen durch modisch designte oder rustikale Belanglosigkeiten. Auch die Gärten sind trendig geworden. Anstelle der Blautanne und des Rhododendronbeetes sind Wildhecke und Magerrasen getreten, geblieben ist die räumliche Indifferenz im quartierübergreifenden Maßstab.

Für die Mathematikerfamilie W. haben die Architekten Schnebli Ammann Ruchat ein beinahe prototypisch einfaches Haus entworfen, das uns an die archaischen Häuser von Kinderzeichnungen erinnert. Die Geometrisierung des Hauses findet im Garten ihre Entsprechung: Das Spiel von Symmetrie und deren feine Abweichungen im Gebäude wird kohärent im Außenraum entwickelt. Die beinahe zentrale Gebäudelage erzeugt auf allen vier Seiten ähnlich geringe Raumtiefen, wobei die paralleloide Grundstücksform durch das rational entwickelte Gartenkonzept thematisiert wird. Das Gebäude steht auf einem Belagsband, dessen Anfang und Ende vom Eingangsplatz und Sitzplatz gebildet werden. Die Längsseiten des Grundstückes werden durch konisch zulaufende, zwei Meter hohe Buchenhecken räumlich gefaßt und damit Ein- und Aussicht begrenzt. Die Geometrisierung der Südgrenze zeigt sich in der exakten Böschung und den darüber gezogenen, schräg ansteigenden Heckenstreifen. Diese sind abwechselnd mit rosa blühenden Chaenomeles und Spireen bepflanzt, Sträucher also, die auch in geschnittener Form ihre Blühfähigkeit bewahren. Mit den Pflanzorten der Bäume wird die Asymmetrie verstärkt, während die Baumzahl und

Without Context: The Love of Geometry

The location and the neighborhood of a property are essential framing conditions for our garden designs. In a few rare cases, the denial of the context is the only sensible way out – and this applies to this case. The scene is a new subdivision of single-family homes in a small community in the Zurich upper land (Oberland). The most notable characteristic of this new quarter is that it doesn't have any outstanding characteristics, or character for that matter, and it fits inconspicuously into the phalanx of hundreds of other such quarters. The gardens also conform to this trend. Instead of the blue fir trees and the rhododendron beds, there are wild hedges and scarce lawns and what remains the same is the spatial indifference on a scale reaching into other quarters.

The architects, Schnebli Ammann Ruchat, have designed an almost prototypical simple home for the family of the mathematician, W., reminding us of the archaic houses in children's drawings. The geometry of the house finds its correspondence in the garden: The play of the symmetry and the subtle irregularities in the building are developed coherently on the outside. The almost central position of the building creates similarly small spatial depths on all four sides, while the paralleled shape of the

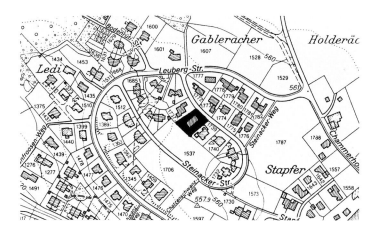

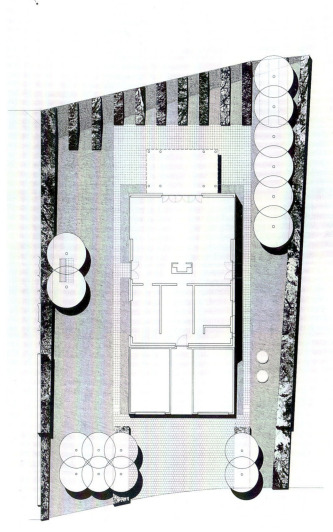

Projektplan 1993
Grundriß, Schnitte
Original 1:50, 60 x 113 cm;
Tusche, Folie, Farbstift
auf Plandruck weiß

Project plan 1993
Ground plan, sections
Original 1:50, 60 x 113 cm;
ink, foil, colored pencil
on white plan print

damit auch das räumliche Gewicht Symmetrie anzeigt. Die acht Weißdornhochstämme signalisieren den transparenten Abschluß zur Straße, der Einblick und Eintritt bewußt zuläßt. Gegenüber der Wohnzimmer-Gartentür sind zwei Japanische Zierkirschen plaziert, zusammen mit der Bank eine Gartenlaube bildend. Eine Reihe eng gestellter Quitten auf der Westseite bildet Sichtschutz für den Balkonsitzplatz gegenüber dem nahe stehenden Nachbarhaus und verweist gleichzeitig auf das noch unüberbaute Gelände im Süden.

Mit den reduziert eingesetzten Elementen gesellt sich zum Haus ein Garten, der seine räumliche und stimmungsmäßige Qualität aus der strengen Geometrie schöpft, die durch Wachstum und Schnitt der Bäume und Hecken erst noch entwickelt werden muß. Im überquellenden Formen- und Materialpotpourri der Nachbarschaft wird aber bereits jetzt deutlich, daß sich unser Ensemble von Haus und Garten loslöst und – eher ungewollt – zum auffälligen Ort der Strenge und Einfachheit geworden ist.

Dieter Kienast

property is taken up as a theme in the rationally developed concept of the garden. The building is placed into a surface strip whose beginning and end are formed by the entrance square and the sitting area. The longitudinal sides of the property are framed spatially by conical two meter high beech hedges which limit the view into and out of the property. The geometry of the southern border shows in the exact slope and the slightly climbing diagonal strips of hedges above the slope. They are planted alternately with rose blossoming Chaenomeles and Spiraeas, bushes which are appreciated for their ability to bloom even when trimmed. The location of the tree plantings enhances the asymmetry, whereas the number of trees and, thus, the spatial weight show a symmetry. The eight high hawthorn bushes signal the transparent conclusion towards the street which consciously allows insights and access. Opposite the living room door to the garden, two Japanese ornamental cherry trees are positioned and together with the bench they form a garden summerhouse. A row of tightly placed quince trees on the west side serves as a visual protection for the terrace towards the close neighboring house and, at the same time, points to the undeveloped grounds to the south.

With the reduced use of elements, the house is joined by a garden which takes its spatial and atmospheric quality from the strict geometry which still has to be further developed with the growth and trimming of the trees and hedges. The overflowing potpourri of forms and materials in the neighborhood makes clear, however, that our ensemble of house and garden is detached and – rather unwittingly – has become an outstanding place of strictness and simplicity.

Dieter Kienast

Im überquellenden Formen- und Materialpotpourri der Nachbarschaft wird aber bereits jetzt deutlich, daß sich unser Ensemble von Haus und Garten loslöst ...

The overflowing potpourri of forms and materials in the neighborhood makes clear, however, that our ensemble of house and garden is detached ...

Die acht Weißdornhochstämme signalisieren den transparenten Abschluß zur Straße, der Einblick und Eintritt bewußt zuläßt. Gegenüber der Wohnzimmer-Gartentür sind zwei Japanische Zierkirschen plaziert ...

The eight high hawthorn bushes signal the transparent conclusion towards the street which consciously allows insights and access. Opposite the living room door to the garden, two Japanese ornamental cherry trees are positioned ...

Nochmals neu

Die Qualität älterer Gärten ist nicht nur in der eingewachsenen Pflanzung begründet, ebenso trägt die angesetzte Patina, die Spuren des langjährigen Gebrauches, Wesentliches zur Stimmung des Ortes bei. Der Rasen hat die aseptische Penetranz der Ansaat verloren, das Staudenbeet zeigt den Übergang zwischen Bestimmtheit und Auflösung und die Betonmauer Variationen von Grautönen und Flechten. Bei Umgestaltungen sind wir deshalb bestrebt, Teile des gealterten, patinierten Gartens zu erhalten.

Unser Garten P. erweist sich bei der ersten Besichtigung als fünf Jahre junger Garten, dem jedoch die Alterungsfähigkeit auch in Zukunft abgeht: fehlende Baumpflanzungen, hunderte von zwergwüchsigen Sträuchern und bereits jetzt verfaulende Böschungseinfassungen aus Baumstämmen.

Ein Neubau des neuen Gartens erschien uns deshalb unumgänglich. Nicht mehr veränderbar war die vom früheren Besitzer angelegte Erschließungsstraße durch den Garten, die diesen unnötig verkleinert und die Entwicklung der Ostseite stark behindert.

Unter Bäumen hindurch gelangen wir auf der Zufahrt zum Eingangshof, der von Buchshecken gesäumt und von der neu gepflanzten Paulownie geprägt wird. Die symme-

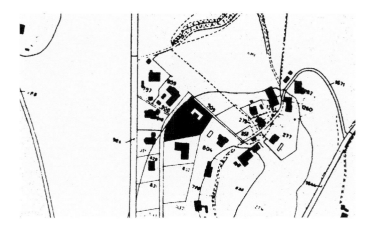

New Again

The quality of older gardens has its origin not only in the mature plantings. It is due also to the acquired patina and the traces of the year-long use that the location acquires a specific atmosphere. The lawn has lost the penetrating aspect of the fresh seeds, the bush bed shows the transition from purposefulness to dissolution and the concrete wall shows variations of gray shades of the growing lichens. We therefore strive, in the case of a redesign, to preserve parts of the aged garden with its patina.

Our garden P. turned out to be only five years old when we first viewed it. But it does not have the potential to age in the future: there are no trees, hundreds of dwarf bushes and slope frames made of logs that have already started to rot. A new design of the garden seemed unavoidable to us. We could not change the access road through the garden which was put in by the former owner and unnecessarily makes it smaller and hinders the development of the east side.

From beneath the trees we reach the entrance yard on the access road framed by box hedges and marked by the newly planted Paulownia tomentosa. The symmetrical U-shape of the building encloses a large sitting area which opens towards the garden. By the use of stepped tree plantings, the spatial axis of the garden is curved with reference to the house and opens up in a window to the further distant hill covered with trees. The west side is limited by a curved yew hedge in front of which is the new swimming pool, covered transparently by the transversely placed bush bed and a layer of Japanese maple trees. And now we wait for the garden to slowly change from new to old with daily use, beneath sun and rain.

Dieter Kienast

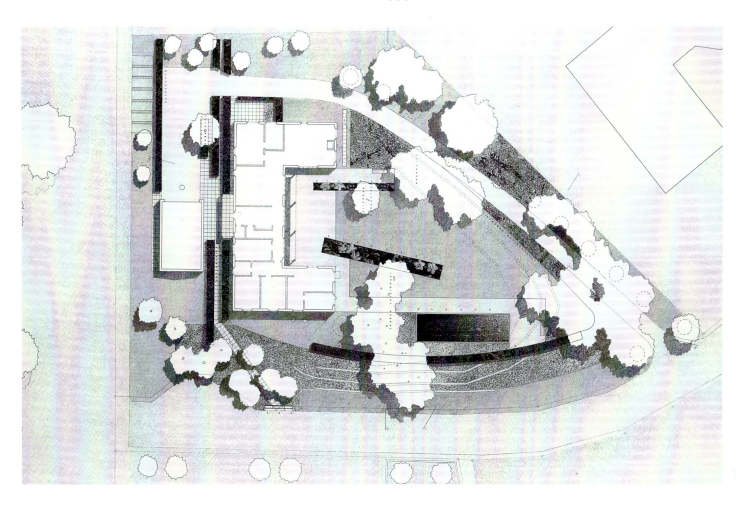

trische U-Form des Gebäudes spannt einen großen Sitzplatz ein, der sich zum Garten hin öffnet. Durch gestaffelte Baumpflanzungen wird die Raumachse des Gartens gegenüber derjenigen des Hauses abgeknickt und öffnet sich in einem Fenster zum weiter entfernt liegenden, baumbestandenen Hügel. Die Westseite ist mit einer gebogenen Eibenhecke begrenzt, vor der das neue Schwimmbecken liegt, transparent verdeckt vom schräg plazierten Staudenbeet und einer Schicht von japanischen Ahornbäumen. Und jetzt warten wir, wie der Garten im alltäglichen Gebrauch, unter Sonne und Regen sich langsam vom Neuen zum Alten entwickelt.

Dieter Kienast

Projektplan 1993
Grundriß
Original 1:100, 70 x 100 cm;
Tusche, Folie, Farbstift
auf Plandruck grau

Project plan 1993
Ground plan
Original 1:100, 70 x 100 cm;
ink, foil, colored pencil
on gray plan print

... gelangen wir auf der Zufahrt zum Eingangshof, der von Buchshecken gesäumt und von der neu gepflanzten Paulownie geprägt wird.

... we reach the entrance yard on the access road framed by box hedges and marked by the newly planted Paulownia tormentosa.

Grenzen und Zäune

Die Englischen Landschaftsgärtner des 18. Jahrhunderts haben mit der Erfindung des Aha's die sichtbaren Grenzen zwischen dem bewußt gestalteten Garten und der bäuerlich bewirtschafteten Landschaft versteckt, aber nicht aufgehoben. Das Bild der arkadischen Hirtenidylle wird im Landschaftsgarten inszeniert, wo es aus der Gebrauchsfähigkeit entlassen ist. Eine feinsinnige Art, Reichtum und Überfluß darzustellen, indem das ärmlich karge Hirtenleben als gebaute Metapher eines glücklich einfachen Daseins in Harmonie mit der Natur vorgezeigt wird. Und nur im Gebrauchsverzicht des Gartens kann die überhöht schöne Hirtenlandschaft Wirklichkeit werden. Zusammen mit dem Einbezug des angrenzenden Landwirtschaftslandes erhält der Garten eine bisher unbekannte inhaltliche und geographische Dimension, die die auf den ersten Blick zur Schau getragene Bescheidenheit der Landedelleute im Zwielicht erscheinen läßt. Mit Hilfe des Aha's wird Landschaft staffagenartig einbezogen. Sie bleibt sowohl als Bild wie als genutzte Landschaft Kulisse auf der Bühne des feinen Lebens im Garten selber. Und nur sie ist letztendlich von Bedeutung.

    Obwohl unser Garten am ehemaligen Bauernhaus ebenfalls die Gunst einer weiträumigen bäuerlichen Um-

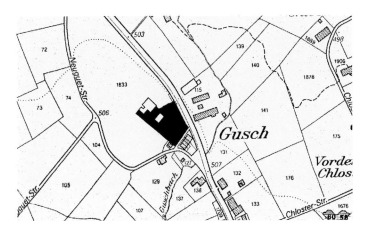

Borders and Fences

The English landscape gardeners of the 18th century, with the invention of the 'ha-ha', have hidden the visible borders between the consciously designed garden and the agriculturally used land. However, they did not entirely do away with them. The picture of the Arcadian ideal of the shepherd is 'staged' in the landscape garden where it is removed from usability. A subtle way to show wealth and surplus is to make the scarce shepherd's life a constructed metaphor of a happy and simple life in harmony with nature. And only by renouncing the usability of the garden can the exaggerated beautiful shepherd's landscape become a reality. Together with the adjoining agricultural land, the garden obtains a dimension, so far unknown in its contents and geography, which puts the modesty of the country noblemen – at first glance pretentious – into a twilight. With the help of the 'ha-ha', the landscape is included in a way of mere display. It remains, as a picture and as a used landscape, a prop on the stage of the noble life in the garden itself. And finally, only this is of any meaning.

    Although our garden at the former farm house also has the advantage of a former wide agricultural surrounding, it shows – with its strictly framed vista windows – a garden approach different from that of the English landscape garden: with bushes, columns, and fence, the border is accentuated. The view of the adjoining orchard is framed by the striking columns and, thus, the difference between the unimportant vista into the landscape and the meaningfully produced outlook is created. Incidentally, the difference between the English and the Swiss landscapes becomes manifest. Whereas it is still widely spread and, therefore, quite ordinary in England, it has become rare in the agglomerate of a big city and is therefore precious because of the archaic style. Between the inside 'farmer's garden' and the outside orchard, the material and formal design of the border points to the new interpretation of the location, which searches for less harmony and more contrast with the agricultural rustic world: concrete columns painted

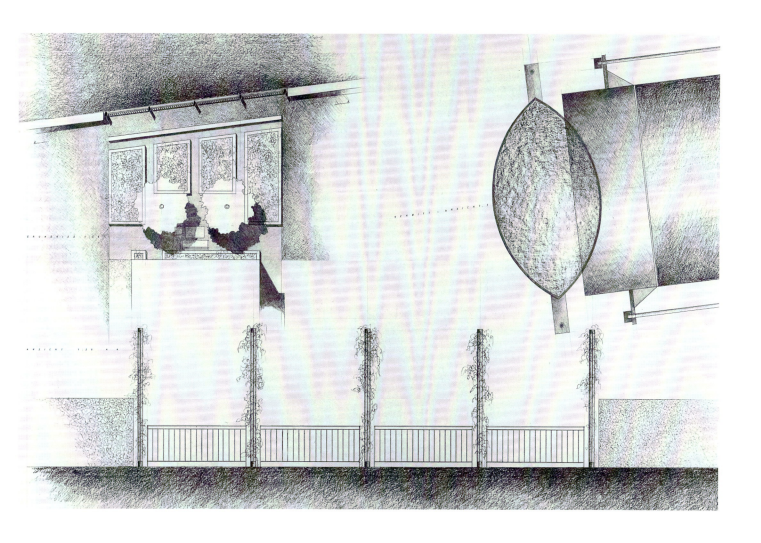

Projektplan 1994
Grundriß, Schnitte
Original 1:50/1:20/1:1, 70 x 100 cm;
Tusche, Farbstift, Ölkreide
auf Plandruck

Project plan 1994
Ground plan, sections
Original 1:50/1:20/1:1, 70 x 100 cm;
ink, colored pencil, oil crayon
on plan print

gebung zukommt, zeigt er mit den streng gefaßten Aussichtsfenstern eine – zum Englischen Landschaftsgarten – differente Gartenauffassung: Mit Hecke, Säulen und Geländer wird die Grenze akzentuiert. Der Blick auf die angrenzende Obstbaumwiese wird mit den markanten Säulen gerahmt und damit die Differenz vom beiläufigen Blick in die Landschaft zur bedeutungsvoll inszenierten Aussicht festgeschrieben. Nebenbei wird damit auch die Differenz zwischen der englischen und schweizerischen Bauernlandschaft manifest. Während in England immer noch weitverbreitet und damit gewöhnlich, ist sie in der Agglomeration der Großstadt selten und gerade in der archaischen Ausprägung kostbar geworden. Zwischen dem inliegenden ‹Bauerngarten› und der außenliegenden Obstwiese verweist die materielle und formale Ausbildung der Grenze auf die neue Interpretation des Ortes, die weniger Harmonie als vielmehr Kontrast zur bäuerlich rustikalen Welt sucht: Grau eingefärbte Betonsäulen mit Chromstahldrähten für die Berankung mit unterschiedlichen Clematisarten und dazwischen ein industriell gefertigter Metallzaun über einer Betonplatte, als Schwelle und Begrenzung des Wieslandes zum sorgfältig gepflegten Gartenrasen.

Den gesamten Garten hat die Besitzerin im Verlauf von zwanzig Jahren Stück für Stück neu gebaut, umgestaltet und bepflanzt. Deutlich erkennbar sind die englischen Vorbilder des Edwardianischen Gartens mit der klaren, architektonischen Grundstruktur und den großflächigen, sorgfältig abgestimmten Staudenpflanzungen. Auf gemeinsamen Spaziergängen durch den Garten wurden Vorzüge und Probleme einzelner Bereiche diskutiert, nach Lösungen gesucht und anschließend umgesetzt. Im Verlaufe der Zeit hat sich Nicole Newmark von der begeisterten Hobbygärtnerin zur passionierten Gartenarchitektin entwickelt und sich ein eigenes Gartenreich geschaffen, dessen Pflanzungen den Vergleich mit ihren englischen Vorbildern nicht zu scheuen brauchen. Und so verspüren wir an diesem Ort etwas gleichermaßen Vertrautes und doch so wenig Selbstverständliches – Gartenkultur.

Dieter Kienast

gray with chrome steel wires for the different types of climbing clematis, and between them an industrially produced metal fence above a concrete platform, as a threshold and limitation from the meadow to the carefully tended garden lawn.

The owner has rebuilt, converted and planted the entire garden in the course of twenty years. The examples of the Edwardian garden with the clear architectural basic structure and the spacious, carefully chosen bushes are clearly visible. During our common walks through the garden we discussed the advantages and problems of various areas, looked for solutions and later on realized them. Within due time, Nicole Newmark has turned from an enthusiastic hobby gardener into a passionate garden architect and has created her own personal garden kingdom whose plantings do not have to shy away from a comparison with their English idols. Thus, we feel something familiar and yet not so self-understood in this place: garden culture.

Dieter Kienast

Grau eingefärbte Betonsäulen mit Chromstahldrähten für die Berankung mit unterschiedlichen Clematisarten und dazwischen ein industriell gefertigter Metallzaun über einer Betonplatte, als Schwelle und Begrenzung des Wieslandes zum sorgfältig gepflegten Gartenrasen.

Concrete columns painted gray with chrome steel wires for the different types of climbing clematis, and between them an industrially produced metal fence above a concrete platform, as a threshold and limitation from the meadow to the carefully tended garden lawn.

Der Blick auf die angrenzende Obstbaumwiese wird mit den markanten
Säulen gerahmt und damit die Differenz vom beiläufigen Blick
in die Landschaft zur bedeutungsvoll inszenierten Aussicht festgeschrieben.

The view of the adjoining orchard is framed by the striking columns and, thus, the difference between the unimportant vista into the landscape and the meaningfully produced outlook is created.

Lob der Zweideutigkeit

Unsichere Zeiten sind angebrochen. Es ist nicht mehr wie früher, sagen uns die alten Leute. Und auch wir spüren, daß scheinbar Unabänderliches, Festgefügtes, Eindeutiges aus den Fugen gerät: die politischen Machtverhältnisse, Religion, Gesellschaft, Familie, Kunst und Natur. Zweierlei Reaktionen sind möglich: das Herbeisehnen des Alten oder die Auseinandersetzung mit der rezenten Unsicherheit. Wir mißtrauen dem restaurativen Gedankengut und fassen das Zeitgeschehen auch in der beruflichen Arbeit als große Chance einer spannenden Entwicklung auf. Wir kultivieren die Freiheit der ambivalenten Wahrnehmung und Interpretation und sind gleichzeitig gegen die Beliebigkeit der Gestalt. Hier streben wir eindeutig Radikalität im Konzept und dessen Umsetzung an.

Der prototypische Garten als umgrenzter Ort definiert sich weniger über die gebaute Grenze als vielmehr durch seine Differenz zwischen Innen und Außen. War früher das Außen mit der Wildnis gleichgesetzt, so treffen wir heute nebenan einen ähnlichen Garten. Unser Grundstück zeigt noch die Nachbarschaft zur Wildnis, mehr noch, das Grundstück ist durch zehnjähriges Brachliegen selbst zur Wildnis geworden. Die vorgefundene Vegetation erzählt uns ihre Geschichte vom periodischen Wechsel zwischen intensivem Gebrauch und Wildwuchs: nitrophile Säume, Kahlschlagfluren, 10 Meter hoher Jungwald und dahinter der 100jährige Wald. Im Jungwald fanden wir verwilderte Gartenstauden, alte Rosenstöcke, Obstgehölz und Beerensträucher.

Die angedeutete Geschichte der Vegetation zeigt Kohärenz zur Kulturgeschichte des Ortes. Wir befinden uns an einem martialischen Ort, in unmittelbarer Nachbarschaft zur größten Festungsanlage Europas, am Rand der tieferliegenden Stadt und des Glacis, der sich zur hochliegenden Burg erstreckt. Das ehemals freie Schußfeld ist zum Wald herangewachsen, das 1877 erbaute Gebäude gehörte dem Wallmeister, der für den Glacisunterhalt zuständig war. Karljosef Schattner und Wilhelm Huber haben den

In Praise of Ambiguity

Uncertain times have begun. Older people tell us that things are no longer as they used to be. And we too can feel that something seemingly unchangeable, fixed and unequivocal is getting out of kilter: the political power structures, religion, society, family, art and nature. Two reactions are possible: the longing for the old or the confrontation of the recent insecurity. We mistrust the restorative ideas and consider the current events a big chance for an exciting development in our professional life, as well. We cultivate the freedom of ambivalent perception and interpretation and at the same time oppose the arbitrary design. Here, we clearly strive for radicalism in the concept and its realization.

The prototypical garden as a fenced-in place defines itself less through the constructed border than through the difference between inside and outside. Whereas in former times the outside was equal to wilderness, today we meet a similar garden right next door. Our property still shows signs of the neighboring wilderness, and, moreover, the property itself has turned into a wilderness after having lain fallow for ten years. The existing vegetation tells us the entire story about the periodic change between intensive use and wild growth: nitrophilous seams, cleared open

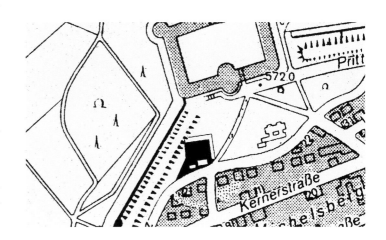

Um- und Neubau für die kulturell engagierten Besitzer geplant.

Der erste Gang durch den dornröschenhaften Garten zeigt alle Reize und Unzulänglichkeiten: Natur ist nicht nur schön, romantisch, vielfältig, sie kann auch banal, indifferent und unattraktiv sein. Der Blick auf die Stadt mit dem Kirchturm und zu den Alpen ist völlig zugewachsen, der Steilhang kaum begehbar.

Ziel und Thematik des Entwurfes ist die präzise Formulierung der drei differenten Erscheinungsformen von Natur, die in Korrespondenz oder Opposition zum Gebauten stehen. Auf der untersten Ebene prägt die gärtnerisch gestaltete Natur das Aussehen der gebäudenahen Gartenteile. Im Steilhang wechseln ruderalisierte und gepflegte Vegetation, während der alte Wald Grenze und Rahmen des inneren Gartens bildet und gleichzeitig den Übergang zur größtmöglichen Naturnähe des äußeren Gartens akzentuiert.

Entlang der Straße bildet die präzis geschnittene Eibenhecke auf der Mauer die Grenze zum Vorgarten und Gartenhof, den Einblick verhindernd und trotzdem Ausblick freilassend. Die Magnolienreihe leitet zum Hauseingang. Die Treppe hochgehend, verwehrt zunächst die Mauer den Einblick in den privaten Hofgarten, der erst nach dem Eintritt ins Treppenhaus überraschend inszeniert wird. In der fein planierten grünen Sandfläche ‹schwimmen› 14, in freien Formen geschnittene Pflanzenfiguren in unterschiedlichen Grüntönen. Beim Nähertreten erkennen wir Buxus, Ilex, Chaenomeles und Azaleen. Die ruhige Formenvariation kontrastiert mit der präzisen Sandebene und den Umgrenzungshecken. In dieser Reduktion wird die Nähe zu japanischen Zen-Gärten deutlich. Ein schmales Wasserbecken markiert die Trennung zwischen den Hausteilen und führt uns gleichzeitig auf die Hinterseite des Hauses, das hier auf einem grünen Andeersplitt-Teppich steht und Distanz zum Steilhang schafft.

Im Steilhang reihen sich Schichten unterschiedlichster Vegetationsbestände, mehrjähriger Ruderal- und Gehölzbestand wechselt mit Strauchreihen, die jeweils nur aus einer Pflanzenart gebildet werden. Diese heben sich in Form, Blüte und Duft deutlich von der Wildvegetation ab:

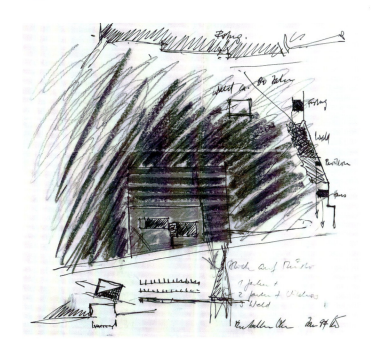

fields, the 10 meter high trees of the young forest and then behind it the century-old forest. In the young forest we found wild garden bushes, old rose bushes, fruit trees and berry bushes.

The mentioned history of the vegetation shows a coherency with the cultural history of the location. We are at a military place, in the immediate neighborhood of the largest fortress in Europe, at the edge of the lower-level city and the glacis stretching towards the castle on the hill. What was formerly an open shooting range has grown into a forest; the building dating back to 1877 belonged to the rampart master who was in charge of the maintenance of the glacis. Karljosef Schattner and Wilhelm Huber planned the conversion and new construction for the culturally engaged owners.

The first walk through the sleeping beauty-like garden reveals all the charms and shortcomings: nature is not only beautiful, romantic and diversified, it can also be banal, indifferent and unattractive. The view of the city with the church tower and the Alps has become completely overgrown and the slope is now hardly accessible.

Konzeptskizze 1994   Conceptual sketch 1994

Parkrosen, Flieder, Amerikanischer Blumenhartriegel, großblumiger Schneeball, Strauchpeonie, Schlehe oder Buchs ziehen sich über die ganze Hangbreite, ohne Rücksicht auf die Topographie und diese gerade dadurch betonend. Die Vegetationsschichten befinden sich im labilen Gleichgewicht zwischen Verwilderung und Kontrolliertheit. So wird manifest, daß unsere ungeteilte Wertschätzung dem Wilden und dem Kultivierten gehört.

Auf der Ostseite führt ein – im Plan auffälliger – Zick-Zackweg zum Aussichtspavillon am höchsten Punkt des Gartens. Die Wegführung ist nicht trendiges Design, sondern vor Ort im Gelände eingepaßt. Sie stellt die sanftest mögliche Höhenüberwindung sicher, analog den Wanderwegen im Gebirge. Der Weg durchschneidet die Vegetationsschichten im Rhythmus differenter Pflanzhöhen und Grüntöne.

Ziel unserer Neugierde ist der oben im Gebüsch leicht versteckte Pavillon mit seiner nicht lesbaren Buchstabenbrüstung. Wir nähern uns dem Pavillon. Eintretend erken-

The goal and theme of the design is the precise phrasing of the three different appearances of nature, which are in correspondence or opposition to the constructed. On the lowest level, the landscaped nature marks the looks of the parts of the garden close to the building. On the slope, the vegetation alternates between the ruderal and the tended, whereas the old forest forms the border and frame for the inside garden and, at the same time, accentuates the transition to the largest possible closeness to nature of the outside garden.

Along the street the precisely trimmed yew hedge along the wall forms the border to the forecourt and garden yard, blocking the view from the outside and yet leaving open an outlook. The row of magnolias leads towards the house entrance. Going up the stairs, the wall denies the view into the private yard garden which is produced, surprisingly, only upon entering the hallway. 14 plant figures trimmed in free forms and showing different shades of green 'float' in the finely leveled green sand surface. At a closer look we recognize Buxus, Ilex, Chaenomeles and azaleas. The calm form variation contrasts with the precise sand plane and the framing hedges. In this reduction, the closeness to Japanese Zen-gardens becomes clear.

A narrow water basin marks the separation between the different parts of the house and leads us at the same time to the back side of the house which stands here on a green Andeer granite gravel-carpet and creates a distance to the steep slope.

On the slope, there are alternating layers of various flora populations, several year old ruderal vegetation, and a copse with rows of bushes, which are also formed by just one type of plant. They clearly differentiate themselves from the wild vegetation in form, flowers and scent: park roses, lilac, American Cornus florida, large flowering snowball, tree peony, sloe and box are spread across the entire width of the slope without consideration for the topography and, in fact, enhancing it. The layers of vegetation are in an unstable balance between wild growth and control. It thus becomes manifest that our unanimous appreciation belongs to both the wild and the cultivated.

Höllenschlund in Bomarzo;
Vicino Orsini, ca. 1560

Hell's gorge in Bomarzo;
Vicino Orsini, approx. 1560

Projektplan 1994 (95)
Grundriß
Original 1:100, 80 x110 cm; Tusche,
Folie, Farbstift auf Plandruck weiß

Ansicht von der Straße

Project plan 1994 (95)
Ground plan
Original 1:100, 80 x 110 cm; ink, foil,
colored pencil on white plan print

View from the street

nen wir einen einfachen Betonrahmen, verstärkt durch die hangseitige, hellgrün eingefärbte Mauer und den talseitigen Schriftzug aus hellblauen Betonbuchstaben. Das gerahmte Bild ist mit Bedeutung aufgeladen: Ganz hinten im Dunst die Alpen, die Stadt mit dem höchsten Kirchturm von Europa, die Pflanzen des Gartens und direkt vor uns «Ogni pensiero vola». Das Bild wirkt gleichzeitig modern und antiquiert. Es verkörpert das Credo visueller Kommunikation, die Gleichwertigkeit von Wort und Bild, erinnert uns aber auch an die Sinnsprüche alter Gärten.

Im heiligen Wald von Bomarzo finden wir die prominentesten Garteninschriften der Renaissance, die von Fürst Orsini als Rätsel und Prüfung der Gelehrtheit seiner Besucher entworfen wurden. Das bekannteste Beispiel findet sich um den Höllenschlund eingehauen – «Ogni pensiero vola». Ein rezenter Irrtum, wie die neuen Nachforschungen von Bredekamp darlegen. Orsini hat das Dante-Zitat aus der Göttlichen Komödie feinsinnig abgewandelt «lasciate ogni pensiero o voi che entrate» – Laßt, die ihr eintretet, jeden Gedanken (und nicht die Hoffnung, wie bei Dante) fahren. In Umkehrung zum fürchterlichen Aussehen des Höllenschlundes entpuppt sich die Höhle in Bomarzo als Ort gemeinsamer Lustbarkeit.

In unserem Garten wird der Irrtum zur Absicht, weil sich auch der Ausdruck nochmals gewandelt hat: Nicht mehr in Nachbarschaft zu steingehauenen Ungeheuern, sondern auf dem höchsten Punkt, über Garten und Stadt, schützt uns der Schriftzug vor dem Absturz und läßt die Gedanken fliegen.

Dieter Kienast

On the east side, a zigzag pathway – standing out on the plan – leads to the outlook pavilion at the highest point in the garden. The path is not a trendy design, but fits into the grounds in situ. It assures the easiest possible ascent of the heights, analogous to the hiking paths in the mountains. The path cuts through the layers of vegetation in the midst of the rhythm of different plant heights and shades of green.

The object of our curiosity is the pavilion with its illegible letter balustrade which is slightly hidden between the shrubbery. We approach the pavilion. Upon entering it we recognize a simple concrete frame, reinforced by the light-green wall of the hillside and the inscription, in light blue concrete letters, on the side of the valley. The framed picture is charged with meaning: all the way back in the haze are the Alps, the city with the highest church tower in Europe, the plants in the garden and directly in front of us, "Ogni pensiero vola". The picture has both a modern and, at the same time, antique effect. It embodies the credo of visual communication, the equality of word and image. It also reminds us of the axioms of old gardens.

In the sacred forest of Bomarzo we find the most prominent garden inscriptions of the Renaissance, which were designed by count Orsini as an enigma and a gesture to the scholarship of his visitors. The most famous example is carved into the hell's gorge – "Ogni pensiero vola". As Bredekamp's new research findings show, this is a piquant error. Orsini has sensitively altered the quote from Dante's Divine Comedy "lasciate ogni pensiero o voi che entrate" – May those who enter let go of every thought (and not hope, as in Dante's case). As an antithesis to the terrible looks of the hell's gorge, the cave in Bomarzo turns out to be a place of common pleasures.

In our garden the error becomes an intention because the expression has changed yet again: removed from the neighborhood of stone-carved monsters, on the highest point above the garden and the city, the inscription protects us from the abyss and allows our thoughts to soar.

Dieter Kienast

Ein schmales Wasserbecken markiert die Trennung zwischen den Hausteilen ... A narrow water basin marks the separation between the different parts of the house ...

In der fein planierten grünen Sandfläche ‹schwimmen› 14,
in freien Formen geschnittene Pflanzenfiguren in unterschiedlichen Grüntönen.
Beim Nähertreten erkennen wir Buxus, Ilex, Chaenomeles und Azaleen.

14 plant figures trimmed in free forms and showing different shades of green 'float' in the finely leveled green sand surface. At a closer look we recognize Buxus, Ilex, Chaenomeles and azaleas.

... verwehrt zunächst die Mauer den Einblick in den privaten Hofgarten, der erst nach dem Eintritt ins Treppenhaus überraschend inszeniert wird.

... the wall denies the view into the private yard garden which is produced, surprisingly, only upon entering the hallway.

Ziel unserer Neugierde ist der oben im Gebüsch leicht versteckte Pavillon mit seiner nicht lesbaren Buchstabenbrüstung.

The object of our curiosity is the pavilion with its illegible letter balustrade which is slightly hidden between the shrubbery.

... wechseln ruderalisierte und gepflegte Vegetation, während der alte Wald Grenze und Rahmen des inneren Gartens bildet und gleichzeitig den Übergang zur größtmöglichen Naturnähe des äußeren Gartens akzentuiert.

... the vegetation alternates between the ruderal and the tended, whereas the old forest forms the border and frame for the inside garden and, at the same time, accentuates the transition to the largest possible closeness to nature of the outside garden.

Eintretend erkennen wir einen einfachen Betonrahmen, verstärkt durch die hangseitige, hellgrün eingefärbte Mauer und den talseitigen Schriftzug aus hellblauen Betonbuchstaben. Das gerahmte Bild ist mit Bedeutung aufgeladen ...

Upon entering it we recognize a simple concrete frame, reinforced by the light-green wall of the hillside and the inscription, in light blue concrete letters, on the side of the valley. The framed picture is charged with meaning ...

Die Wegführung ist nicht trendiges Design, sondern vor Ort im
Gelände eingepaßt. Sie stellt die sanftest mögliche Höhenüberwindung sicher,
analog den Wanderwegen im Gebirge. Der Weg durchschneidet die
Vegetationsschichten im Rhythmus differenter Pflanzhöhen und Grüntöne.

The path is not a trendy design, but fits into the grounds in situ. It assures the easiest possible ascent of the heights, analogous to the hiking paths in the mountains. The path cuts through the layers of vegetation in the midst of the rhythm of different plant heights and shades of green.

Der neue Gartenraum

Geometrie und Zuschnitt von Haus und Grundstück zeigen häufig ein Potential an räumlichen Entwicklungsmöglichkeiten, das in der konkreten Umsetzung nicht ausgeschöpft wird. Die «capabilities» aufzuspüren und daraus Lösungsansätze zu formulieren, ist ein wichtiger Teil unserer planerischen Arbeit.

Das Quartier liegt am Rand der mittelalterlichen Stadt und zeigt zusammengebaute Einzelhäuser und bescheidene Villen, die größtenteils aus dem 19. Jahrhundert stammen. Im Unterschied zur Altstadt haben die Häuser kleine, mit Mauern oder Zäunen eingefriedete, verborgene Gärten. Inmitten dichter Bebauung steigert sich offenbar das Bedürfnis nach unbeobachtetem Rückzugsraum, wie dies in mittelmeerischen Gebieten üblich ist.

Obwohl unsere Liegenschaft als Eckgrundstück ausgezeichnet ist, folgt das Gebäude der Haustypologie an der Plessurstraße, es ist wie die anderen Häuser axial ausgerichtet und reagiert nicht auf die Ecksituation. Umso größer ist deshalb der Gartenzuschnitt. Trotz Verwilderung waren zu Beginn kennzeichnende Reste einer klar konzipierten Anlage festzustellen: Die Hauptachse des Gebäudes wird im Garten mit dem Wasserbecken, der Metallpergola und zwei mächtigen Bäumen fortgeführt. Metallbögen mit Obstspalieren führen auf der Westseite zum Brunnenbecken.

Die Neukonzeption verzichtet auf die weitere Verstärkung der Hauptachse, die zwangsläufig eine Vernachlässigung des östlichen Gartenteiles bedeuten würde. Dieser Gartenteil wird durch die neue Wegführung mit den Raumelementen Hecke und Clematisgang zum bedeutsamen Bereich des Gesamtgartens. Die jetzt noch niederen Eibenhecken verhindern zukünftig den Einblick von der Straße und fassen den Gartenraum prägnant. Von der Sitzbank aus erleben wir eine überraschend neue räumliche Komposition von Garten und Gebäude, wobei das Haus nicht mehr Mittelpunkt des Gartens, sondern vielmehr als flankierendes Gebäude einer Raumfolge wahrgenommen wird, die sich über die Grundstücksgrenze hinaus in die

The New Garden Space

Geometry and layout of house and property often show a potential of spatial development which is not exhausted in the concrete realization. Finding these capabilities and phrasing solutions from them is an important part of our planning work.

The quarter is located at the edge of the medieval city and presents row houses and modest villas largely dating back to the 19th century. Contrary to the old part of the city, the houses have small hidden gardens surrounded by walls or fences. In the midst of a dense development, the need for unobserved space to withdraw obviously increases, as is usually the case in Mediterranean regions.

Although our property is registered as a corner lot, the building follows the house typology at Plessurstrasse and, like all other houses, has an axial orientation and does not react to the corner situation. Therefore, the garden layout is even larger. Despite the wild growth, we could see the remnants of a clearly designed complex: the main axis of the building is continued in the garden with the water basin, the metal pergola and two mighty trees. Metal arcs with fruit trellises lead to the fountain basin on the west side.

The new conception renounces the further enhancement of the main axis, which would inevitably mean a ne-

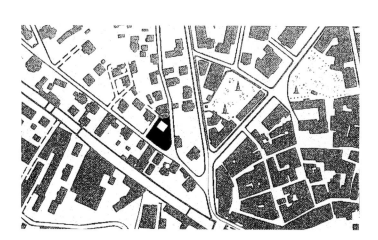

137

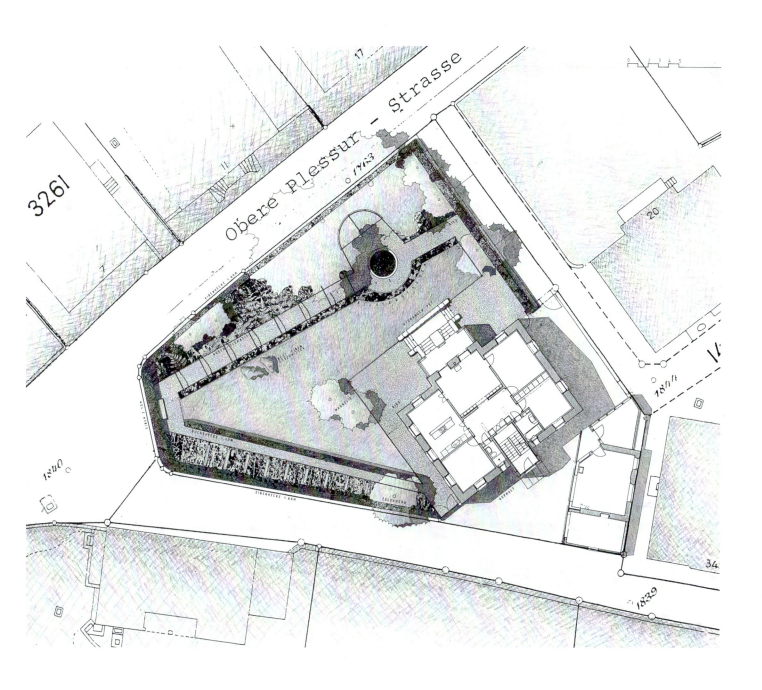

Projektplan 1993
Grundriß
Original 1:50, 50 x 70 cm;
Tusche, Folie, Farbstift auf
Großxerox weiß

Project plan 1993
Ground plan
Original 1:50, 50 x 70 cm;
ink, foil, colored pencil
on white Xerox copy

Nachbargärten fortsetzt. Das Ecksegment des Gartens ist als ruhige Rasenfläche mit zwei Magnolien und einer skulptural geschnittenen Eibengruppe ausgebildet. In den Seitensegmenten sind Stauden- und Gemüsebeete angeordnet. Die vorhandenen alten Elemente Brunnen, Pergola und Sitzplatz wurden renoviert.

Mit der neuen Entwicklung des Ecksegmentes und dem vorhandenen axialen Gartenteil wird nicht nur eine scheinbare Vergrößerung des Gartens erreicht, das Ensemble hat auch eine neue Komplexität gewonnen.

Dieter Kienast

glect of the eastern part of the garden. This part becomes the meaningful area of the entire garden with the new lead of the pathway and the Clematis passage. The yew hedges, which are still small at this point, will block the view from the street in the future and poignantly frame the garden. From the sitting bench we experience a surprisingly new spatial composition of garden and building, while the house is no longer perceived as the focal point of the garden, but rather as a flanking building in a spatial sequence that continues beyond the property border into the neighboring gardens. The corner segment of the garden is a placid lawn surface with two magnolias and a sculpturally trimmed group of yews. Bush and vegetable beds are laid out in the side segments. The existing old elements, the fountain, pergola and sitting area were renovated.

The new development of the corner segment and the existing axial part of the garden not only creates an apparent enlargement of the garden, but the ensemble has also gained a new complexity.

Dieter Kienast

Dieser Gartenteil wird durch die neue Wegführung mit den Raumelementen Hecke und Clematisgang zum bedeutsamen Bereich des Gesamtgartens. Die jetzt noch niederen Eibenhecken verhindern zukünftig den Einblick ...

This part becomes the meaningful area of the entire garden with the new lead of the pathway and the Clematis passage. The yew hedges, which are still small at this point, will block the view ...

Monsieur Hulot im Garten

Erinnern Sie sich noch, wie das Haus des Schwagers im Film «Mon oncle» ausgesehen hat? Sehen Sie, ich auch nicht. Nachhaltig geblieben sind aber die Gartenbilder: die hohe Mauer, der Springbrunnen mit dem Fisch, der nur sprudelt, wenn besondere Gäste kommen. Oder die merkwürdige Wegführung, bei der man überall hinkommt, nur nicht zum anvisierten Ziel, der allzu kleine Sitzplatz, von dem aus man unweigerlich ins Blumenbeet tritt, ganz zu schweigen von der schütteren Bepflanzung der Blumenbeete. Und dazwischen – kreuz und quer – Hulot: verwirrt, mit federndem Schritt und der steil angestellten Pfeife im Mund im ebenso heftigen wie nutzlosen Versuch, dem exaltiert aussehenden Garten eine halbwegs vernünftige Nutzung abzugewinnen. Ungewöhnliches Design – so wäre eine Interpretation – steht dem Alltagsgebrauch entgegen. Von Hulot lernen wir aber auch, wie kleinster Raum unsere Aufmerksamkeit in Anspruch nehmen kann: Mit dem Blick nach unten zum schmalen und verwinkelten Weg gerichtet, wird der Gang durch den Garten überraschend und weit. Erlebbare Größe ist demnach nicht eine Frage der Anzahl Quadratmeter, sie wird über das Maß unterschiedlicher Wahrnehmungen bestimmt. Im weiteren macht uns Hulot darauf aufmerksam, daß der Film das adäquate Medium der Gartendarstellung ist, sei es in der Bewegungsabfolge oder den nachgeschalteten Standbildern.

    Vielleicht zeigt der Garten B. auf den ersten Blick tatieske Züge: anstelle quartiersüblicher, gepflegter Langeweile von Haus und Garten, eine Betonmauer mit Fensterausblick, ein symmetrischer Hausanbau ohne dazugehörige Gartenraum-Tiefe, Hecken in Rasenhöhe, aufrecht stehende Bretter und große Belagsflächen aus grün gefärbtem Beton. Der zweite Blick verrät, daß nicht Clownerie, sondern Reaktion auf schwierige Randbedingungen gemeint ist, allenfalls mit einem spitzbübischen Augenzwinkern.

    Von der Quartierstraße herkommend, sozusagen durch den Hintereingang, wird ein erstaunlicher Garteneintritt inszeniert. ‹Nur sitzen› wie Loriot und dabei die überra-

Monsieur Hulot in the Garden

Do you remember the house of the brother-in-law in the movie "Mon oncle"? You see. I don't either. However, the pictures of the garden have stuck in my mind: the high wall, the fountain with the fish that only bubbles if special guests arrive, the strange lead of the pathway that takes you everywhere except the place you have in mind, the much too small sitting area from where you unavoidably step into the flower bed, and, not to mention, the thin planting of the flower beds. And amidst all this – crisscross – Hulot: confused, with a springy walk and the pipe sharply rising from his mouth, attempting desperately and in vain to get some kind of reasonable use out of the exalted garden. An unusual design – this would be one interpretation – is apposed to the every-day-use. We can also learn from Hulot how the smallest space is able to catch our attention: the view directed down to the small and curvy pathway, the walk through the garden becomes surprising and wide. The experience of size is, therefore, not a question of the number of square meters. It is determined by the scale of various perceptions. Further along, Hulot points out to us that film is the adequate medium for presenting a garden, be it in the sequence of movement or the following still pictures.

    Perhaps the garden B. shows Tatiesque characteristics at first glance. Instead of the well-tended boredom of house and garden that is usual in this quarter, there is a concrete wall with a window, a symmetrical house extension without any garden space depth, hedges by of the lawn, vertical boards and large surface areas made of green concrete. A second glance reveals that the intention is not a clowning around. Instead, it is a reaction to the difficult conditions with, at most, a mischievous wink.

    Coming from the quarter street, so to speak, through the back door, an amazing entrance to the garden is produced. Just sit there – like Loriot (a German comedian) – and take in the surprising depth of the garden space running cross to the house. The spatial depth is not attained by

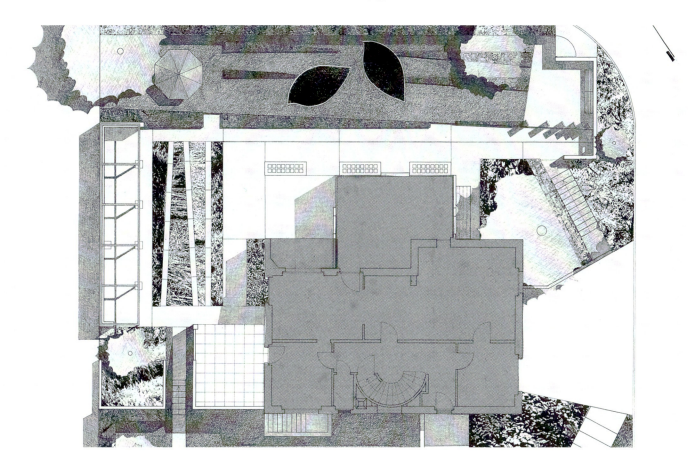

schende Tiefe des quer zum Haus gestellten Gartenraumes aufnehmend. Raumtiefe wird hier nicht durch großzügiges Leerlassen, sondern durch Aufmerksamkeit, durch weitere Unterbrechung erreicht. Die schmale Rasenfläche wird durch konische Buchshecken weiter unterteilt, über spiegelnde Wasserblätter geht der Blick zum Gegenüber, einem alten Gartenpavillon. Grüntöne verschiedenster Konsistenz – Magnolie, Eibe, Buchs, Rasen und Beton. Die Thymianpunkte in der Kiesrinne führen zum Staudenbeet, zur alten Glyzinenpergola und wieder zurück. Unter mehrmaligem Hutheben bedankt sich Hulot bei Familie B., findet ohne Umwege den Treppenausgang und blickt noch einmal nachdenklich zurück – Alchemilla und Beton präsentieren sich erstaunlich gut.

Erika Kienast-Lüder

generous empty spaces, but by the attention and more interruption. The narrow lawn area is divided up even more by conical box hedges, and the view, gliding over reflecting leaves of water, reaches the opposite, an old garden pavilion. Shades of green of most various consistency – magnolia, yew, box, lawn and concrete. The thyme patches in the gravel groove lead to the border of shrubs, to the old Wisteria sinensis pergola and back again. Lifting his hat several times, Hulot says his thanks to the family B., directly finds his way to the stair exit, and again looks back, wondering – Alchemilla and concrete do present themselves amazingly well.

Erika Kienast-Lüder

Projektplan 1994
Grundriß
Original 1:50, 78 x 78 cm;
Tusche, Folie, Farbstift auf Plandruck weiß

Project plan 1994
Ground plan
Original 1:50, 78 x 78 cm;
ink, foil, colored pencil on white plan print

... Eibe, Buchs, Rasen und Beton. Die Thymianpunkte in der Kiesrinne führen zum Staudenbeet, zur alten Glyzinenpergola und wieder zurück.

... yew, box, lawn and concrete. The thyme patches in the gravel groove lead to the border of shrubs, to the old Wisteria sinensis pergola and back again.

Unter mehrmaligem Hutheben bedankt sich Hulot bei Familie B., findet ohne Umwege den Treppenausgang und blickt noch einmal nachdenklich zurück – Alchemilla und Beton präsentieren sich erstaunlich gut.

Lifting his hat several times, Hulot says his thanks to the family B., directly finds his way to the stair exit, and again looks back, wondering – Alchemilla and concrete do present themselves amazingly well.

Beinahe im Wald

In fast allen von uns geplanten Gärten müssen wir nicht bei Stand Null – auf der grünen Wiese – beginnen. Es ist immer bereits ‹etwas da›: Einmal ist es ein markanter Baum, eine spannungsvolle Topografie, eine gute Aussicht, das andere Mal finden wir einen bestehenden Garten vor, mit dem die Bewohner nicht zufrieden sind. Es ist unser erklärtes Ziel, mit möglichst wenigen Eingriffen einen «guten Garten» herzustellen. Dabei begründen sich die wenigen Eingriffe nicht aus einer bewußt asketischen Haltung. Vielmehr ist es die Erkenntnis, daß die meisten Orte aufgrund ihrer Größe oder besser ihrer Begrenztheit keine allzugroße Fülle an Themen und Elementen zulassen, ohne überladen zu wirken.

Zum Hauptthema dieses Gartens wird die Entwicklung einer präzisen Topografie. Unser kleiner Garten besteht aus vielen kleinen Gartenteilen, die auf unterschiedlichen Terrainebenen rund um das bemerkenswerte Gebäude aus den 50er Jahren angeordnet sind. Vom bekannten Architekten Rudolf Steiger erbaut, orientiert sich das aufgeständerte Wohnhaus am Steilhang zum Bachtobel mit eindrucksvollem, altem Waldbestand. Der Wald ist sowohl aus dem Gebäudeinnern als auch von den einzelnen Gartenteilen her omnipräsent, nur gegen Westen wird der Blick frei auf das Nachbargebäude, Stadt und See. Die gartenarchitektonische Intervention zielt auf die differente Ausformulierung der Teilgärten, die von ihrer Terrain- bzw. Gebäudezuordnung in drei Teile getrennt werden: Der Steilhang vom Gehsteig zum Eingang, Ost- und Westgarten zum 1. Wohngeschoß und Garten zum 2. Wohngeschoß. Als Zusammenfassung und Verbindung der drei Gartenteile wird die westliche Grenzhecke bestimmt, die mit dem Terrain verläuft und 2,20 Meter hoch ist. Die Hecke ist als geschnittene Mischhecke konzipiert, deren Artenzusammensetzung derjenigen des angrenzenden Waldes entspricht: Fagus, Carpinus, Acer, Viburnum, Crataegus etc. Die Hecke stellt somit das Extrakt des Waldes in gärtnerisch kontrollierter Form dar. Die parallel zum Hang

Almost in the Forest

In almost all of the gardens we plan, we don't have to start from scratch. There is always 'something there' already: one time it is a striking tree, a topography full of suspense, a nice view; the next time we find an existing garden that does not meet the approval of its owners. It is our proclaimed goal to create a 'good garden' with as few operations as possible. The few operations are not based, however, on a consciously ascetic attitude. Moreover, it is the realization that most places do not allow a large scale of themes and elements due to their size or their limitations without having an overloaded effect.

This garden's main theme is the development of a precise topography. Our small garden consists of many small parts which are arranged around the remarkable '50s building on various levels in the terrain. Erected by Rudolf Steiger, the famous architect, the post and beam house is oriented towards the steep slope by the valley with the brook with an impressive old forest. The forest is omnipresent in the inside of the building as well as the various garden parts and only towards the west does one have a view of the neighboring building, the city and the lake. The goal of the architectural garden intervention is the different phrasing of the partial gardens which are separated into three sections due to their situation in the terrain, or with reference to the building: the steep slope from the walkway to the entrance, the east and west side garden to the first living floor and the garden to the second floor. The hedge on the western border is determined to be a summary and connection of the three garden parts. It follows the terrain and has a height of 2.20 meters. It has been conceived as a mixed trimmed hedge whose composition of species corresponds to that of the adjoining forest: Fagus, Carpinus, Acer, Viburnum, Crataegus, etc. Thus, the hedge represents an extract of the forest in the controlled form of a garden. The stepped levels of the slope in the form of walls and steep inclines are accentuated with unified Tilia and Taxus hedges planted in front.

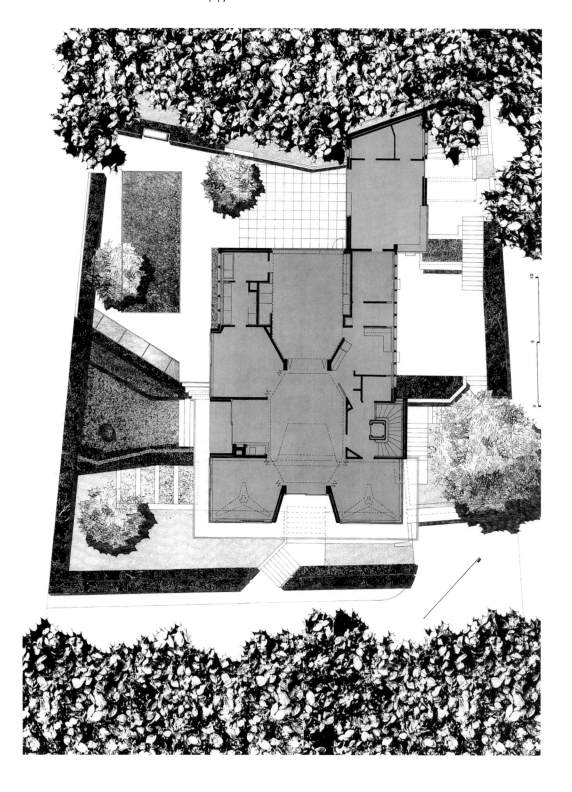

Projektplan 1993
Grundriß
Original 1:50, 70 x 96 cm;
Tusche, Folie, Farbstift
auf Plandruck weiß

Project plan 1993
Ground plan
Original 1:50, 70 x 96 cm;
ink, foil, colored pencil
on white plan print

verlaufenden Höhensprünge in Form von Mauern oder Steilböschungen werden mit vorgepflanzten, einheitlichen Tilia- und Taxushecken akzentuiert.

Entlang des Gehsteiges bildet eine Doppelhecke mit weiß blühenden Chaenomeles und Liguster den Abschluß und Sockel des steil ansteigenden Hanges, der mit Efeu und Farnen bepflanzt und in dem ein kleiner Gemüsegarten eingelagert ist. Dem ersten Wohngeschoß ist auf der Ostseite der große Kiesplatz zugeordnet, direkt vor der Küche liegend ist er als Frühstücksplatz bestens geeignet. Drei Stufen tiefer liegt der Westgarten, als gespannte Rasenfläche mit skulptural geschnittenem Buchs ausgebildet.

Der größte der kleinen Gartenteile ist dem zweiten Wohngeschoß zugeordnet. Ursprünglich als schräg abfallender Gartenteil mit einem allzu bescheidenen Sandsteinmäuerchen als unterem Abschluß versehen, wurde die Verwandtschaft zum beliebigen Wohngartenstil der 30er und 40er Jahre deutlich, der jedoch der kraftvollen Klarheit der Architektur kaum entsprochen hat.

Durch Erhöhung der vorderen Abschlußmauer und Abgrabung der hinteren Böschung wird eine horizontale Ebene eingeführt, die scheinbar direkt an den Wald grenzt. Die Abbruchkante des Gartens ist mit einem schmalen Wasserbecken gefaßt. Die gespannte Gartenebene findet mit dem Materialwechsel von Wasser zu Kies einen präzisen Abschluß, der gleichzeitig den Blick weiterleitet. Im Kiesbelag eingeschnitten liegt vertieft – einem grünen Teppich gleich – ein rechteckiges Rasenstück, das mit seiner klaren Geometrie die Schrägen des Gartenstückes hervorhebt. Im Frühjahr zeichnen die geometrisch gepflanzten Narzissen vorerst noch das Rasenrechteck nach, im Verlauf der Jahre wird die Strenge der Pflanzung durch freiere Gruppierungen abgelöst. Auf der Bank sitzend, erkennen wir linkerhand die Terrasse mit dem prächtigen Cornus kousa, vor uns das Rasenstück mit dem – die Asymmetrie betonenden – jungen Cornus und dem rostroten Strich des Wasserbeckens, in dem sich der scheinbar direkt dahinterliegende Wald bruchstückhaft spiegelt. Nähe und Distanz gebauter und gewachsener Welt verdichten sich zu einem gleichzeitig spanunngsvollen und ruhigen Ort.

Dieter Kienast

Along the walkway a double hedge of white flowering Chaenomeles and Ligustrum (privet) forms the termination and base of the steeply rising hill which is planted with ivy and fern and has a small vegetable garden incorporated into it. On the east side of the first floor we find the large gravel square which, being located directly outside the kitchen, is perfectly suitable as a place for having breakfast. The west garden is three steps lower and consists of a wide lawn surface with sculpturally trimmed box.

The largest of the small garden sections is assigned to the second floor. Originally it was a slanted part with a small and all-too-modest limestone wall as a lower termination point. When it was contrived, the relationship to the garden style of the '30s and '40s was clear, but it hardly corresponded to the powerful clarity of the architecture.

By raising the termination wall in the front and leveling off the slope in the back, a horizontal level is being introduced which seems to adjoin the forest. The edge of the garden is framed with a small water basin. The wide garden level finds a precise termination in the change of material, from gravel to water which, at the same time, continues to guide the view further on. Cut into the gravel lies a rectangular, lowered piece of lawn – similar to a green carpet – which enhances the sloped lines of the garden section with its clear geometry. In the springtime, the geometrically planted narcissus redraw the lawn rectangle. During the course of the year, the strictness of the plantings is relieved by more liberated groupings of plants. Sitting on the bench, we recognize to our left the terrace with its glorious Cornus kousa. Directly in front of us is the piece of lawn with the young Cornus – enhancing the asymmetry – and the rusty red line of the water basin where the adjoining forest, which seems almost directly wedded to the garden, is fragmentarily reflected. Closeness and distance of the built and grown world condense into a place which is simultaneously full of tension and calm.

Dieter Kienast

... jungen Cornus und dem rostroten Strich des Wasserbeckens,
in dem sich der scheinbar direkt dahinterliegende Wald bruchstückhaft spiegelt.
Nähe und Distanz gebauter und gewachsener Welt verdichten sich ...

... the young Cornus and the rusty red line of the water basin where the adjoining forest, which seems almost directly wedded to the garden, is fragmentarily reflected. Closeness and distance of the built and grown world condense ...

Der Außenraum muß ein sinnlicher Ort sein

Die schmale, fensterlose Straßenfront des zweistöckigen Wohngebäudes, die Radikalität der makellos weißen Hauswand und die darunter abtauchende Garageneinfahrt heißen den Ankömmling nicht gerade mit offenen Armen willkommen. Nur ein enger, von Mauern gefaßter kurzer Treppenlauf nach oben deutet auf einen Zugang hin. Der Blick richtet sich auf die bizarre Gestalt einer Robinie, die dem überragenden Kubus des Obergeschosses ausweicht und ihr filigranes Geäst vor kühl reflektierenden Glasflächen rahmenloser Fenster ausbreitet.

‹Strenge allein kann sehr dogmatisch sein.›[1]

Die schweren, 1 x 1 Meter großen Bodenplatten aus Beton rücken entlang der Westfassade eine Handbreit auseinander und bieten dem Frauenmantel genug Lebensraum, um in einer durchgehend längsgerichteten Fuge sein fächerförmiges Blattwerk zu entfalten. Der zartgrüne Streifen weist den Weg zum Garten, dem eine vorhandene Thujaheckenwand den strengen Rahmen verleiht. In ihrem Schutz entwickelt sich in einer zweiten Schicht die Buchenhecke, die bald ihr jahreszeitlich sommergrünes Spiel mit dem dunklen Immergrün der Thujen spielen wird.

«Wir wünschten uns einen fröhlichen Garten, der blühen und duften sollte, ein Revier zum Erholen, einen meditativen Ort und keine überbordende Fülle aus Farben und Formen»[2]

Das präzise Layout des Gartens steht in deutlichem Bezug zum markanten architektonischen Ausdruck des von Herzog & de Meuron umgebauten Wohnhauses aus den frühen dreißiger Jahren. Fast wie bei einem wissenschaftlichen Meßgerät wird die Natur durch Architektur und Gartenstruktur ablesbar. Zugleich spiegelt die Gartengestaltung in ihrer strikten Reduktion der Formensprache jene konstituierenden Merkmale der klassischen Moderne wieder, denen bereits das

The Outside Space must be a Sensual Place

The narrow, windowless street front of the two-story apartment house and the radically spotless white wall of the house with the garage entrance diving down beneath it do not really welcome the visitor with open arms. Only a short, narrow staircase framed by walls points to an access. The view is directed to the bizarre shape of a robinia, which avoids the towering cube of the upper floor and spreads its filigree branches in front of the cool, reflecting glass surfaces of unframed windows.

'Strictness alone can be very dogmatic'[1]

The large, 1 x 1 meter concrete floor tiles along the west facade are a hand width apart and offer enough living space for the lady's mantle to develop its fan-shaped leaves in a longitudinal joint. The light green strip points to the garden access which is given its strict framing by an existing thuja hedge wall. Under its cover the beech hedge develops in a second layer and soon it will begin its seasonal summer 'green play' with the dark evergreen of the thujas.

"We wished for a happy garden which would be flowering and have a nice scent, an area for recuperating, a

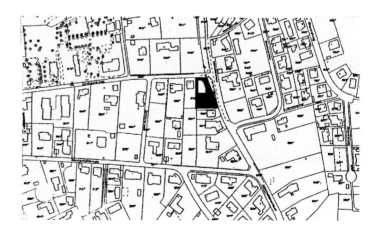

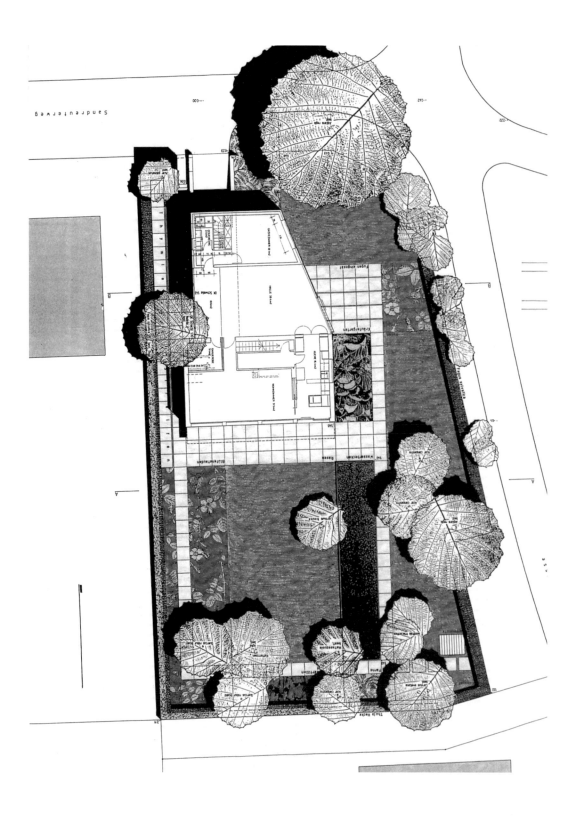

Projektplan 1995
Grundriß
Original 1:100, 50 x 60 cm;
Tusche, Folie, Farbstift
auf Großxerox weiß

Project plan 1995
Ground plan
Original 1:100, 50 x 60 cm;
ink, foil, colored pencil
on white Xerox copy

ursprüngliche Architektur- und Gartenkonzept des Basler Architekten und Bauhausschülers Rudolf Preiswerk verpflichtet war. Der orthogonal geführte Plattenweg rahmt eine nahezu quadratische, etwa 225 Quadratmeter große Fläche ein, die in drei unterschiedlich breite, rechteckige Segmente geteilt ist: Wasserbecken, Rasen und ein Feld mit Blütenstauden, bepflanzt im rational streifenförmigen Schema.

› Die Anreicherung des Raumes geschieht von selbst, während wir Sorge tragen müssen, den tragfähigen Rahmen zu schaffen ›

«Nicht zuletzt wegen unseres medizinischen Berufes liegt uns das strukturierte Denken sehr nahe.»

Im Lauf der Zeit erwacht die Strenge zum Leben: Die Blütenpracht in weiß und blau, das zarte Rot der Rosen und das üppige Wachstum in variantenreichem Grün durchbricht die scheinbare Statik der architektonischen Grundkonzeption. Die exakte Tuschlinie im Plan des Gartenarchitekten wird plötzlich als abstraktes Konstrukt entlarvt, wirkt ordnend, nicht nötigend.

‹Das Chaos müssen wir nicht erzeugen, weil es von selbst ensteht›

Schwere, 30 Zentimeter hohe U-Stahlträger spannen in exakt waagerechter Lage den verschweißten, 15 Meter langen und 3 Meter breiten Rahmen eines Wasserbeckens auf. Dieser erinnert an die frühen Skulpturen «Untitled» des amerikanischen Minimalisten Robert Morris. Der dunkle Wasserspiegel reicht haarscharf unter die Oberkante des rostroten bis schwärzlichen Rohstahls, er wirkt wie ein rahmenloser Spiegel im Garten und erfaßt seismographisch die Lebendigkeit seiner Umgebung: Windhauch, Froschsprung, Seerosenblüte, Kerzenlicht, Libellenflug, Blütenregen, Laubfall, Herbstfrost, Schneedecke.

«Als wir am Abend nach Hause kamen stellten wir fest, daß das Geschehen des Tages vom Wasser registriert worden war. Blätter und Zweige trieben auf der Oberfläche»

meditative place not overdone with an overabundance of colors and shapes."[2]

The precise layout of the garden is a clear reference to the striking architectural expression of the early '30s house converted by Herzog & de Meuron. Similar to a scientific measuring device, nature can be read through the architecture and structure of the garden. At the same time, the garden design in its strict reduction of the form language reflects the constituting characteristics of classical modernism to which the original architecture and garden concept of the Basle architect and Bauhaus student Rudolf Preiswerk was already dedicated. The orthogonal tile path frames an area that is almost square, a 225 square meter area which is divided into three square segments of differing widths: water basin, lawn, and a field with flowering shrubs planted in the rational stripe pattern scheme.

'The enrichment of space happens by itself, while we have to take care of creating the structural framework.'

"Due to our profession we are very close to the structured thinking."

In the course of time, the strictness comes to life: the wealth of white and blue flowers, the soft red of the roses and the buoyant growth in rich variations of green breaks through the seemingly static character of the basic architectural concept. The precise ink line of the garden architect's plan is suddenly revealed to be an abstract construct and has an effect of order and not of force.

'We don't have to create chaos because it creates itself.'

Heavy U-beam steel supports of 30 cm height mounted in a precise horizontal position redraw the 15 by 3 meter welded frame of a water basin. It reminds one of the early "Untitled" sculptures by the American minimalist, Robert Morris. The mirroring surface of the dark water reaches just up to the upper edge of the rusty red to black raw steel and

Der Blick richtet sich auf die bizarre Gestalt einer Robinie, die dem überragenden Kubus des Obergeschosses ausweicht und ihr filigranes Geäst vor kühl reflektierenden Glasflächen rahmenloser Fenster ausbreitet.

The view is directed to the bizarre shape of a robinia, which avoids the towering cube of the upper floor and spreads its filigree branches in front of the cool, reflecting glass surfaces of unframed windows.

Nahe beim Becken, unweit der markanten Linie wo sich Rostrot und Grasgrün begegnen, entfaltet ein einzelner Blütenhartriegel im Juni seine schlichten weißen Blüten. Er bildet den zentralen Blickpunkt des Gartens während der üpppige Bestand vorhandener Bäume den Gartenraum großzügig umrahmt.

› Die Gestaltung von Außenräumen ist zunächst eine relativ einfache Aufgabe. Manchmal reduzieren sich die Dinge einfach auf den rechten Baum am rechten Ort. Schwierigkeiten entstehen erst mit dem Versuch, einen besondern Ort zu schaffen‹

Unter dem Küchenfenster an der südöstlichen Ecke des Hauses verströmen die Gewürzpflanzen des kleinen Kräutergartens ihren aromatischen Duft in der Vormittagssonne, während sich die große Halle des Hauses mit ihrer hohen Glasfront gegen Nordosten dem schattigen Farngarten zuwendet. Ein grüner Schimmer erfüllt den feierlichen, über zwei Geschosse reichenden Hallenraum. Innen und Außen verbinden sich zu einem stimmungsvollen Ganzen, und dennoch signalisiert der harte Kontrast zwischen dem dunklen Schiefergrau des inneren und dem hellen Betongrau des äußeren Plattenbelages eine Transparenz, die das Verwischen der Grenzen bewußt unterbindet.

«Ich flüchte mich im Sommer vor der Hitze der Mittagssonne bevorzugt in die Kühle des Farngartens, durch den fast immer ein leichter Wind weht. Hier fühle ich mich an einen geheimen Waldort erinnert.»

› Der Außenraum muß ein sinnlicher Ort sein.‹

Udo Weilacher

---

[1] Alle einfach angeführten Zitate stammen aus einem Gespräch mit Dieter Kienast im Sommer 1995.
[2] Alle doppelt angeführten Zitate stammen aus einem Gespräch mit Familie L. im Frühjahr 1996.

seems to be a frameless mirror in the garden, seismographically taking in the liveliness of its surroundings: a breath of air, the leap of a frog, the blossom of a sea rose, candle light, the flight of a dragon fly, blossom rain, foliage, the first frost in fall, the blanket of snow.

"When we came home in the evening, we discovered that the events of the day had been captured by the water. Leaves and branches were floating on the surface."

Near the basin, close to the striking line where rusty red and grass green meet, a single Cornus florida unfolds its simple white blossoms in June. It is the central focal point in the garden, while the population of existing trees generously frames the garden space.

'The design of outside spaces is at first a relatively simple task. Sometimes things simply reduce to the right tree in the right location. It only gets difficult if you attempt to create a special place.'

Beneath the kitchen window on the south eastern corner of the house, the herbs in the small spice garden spread their aroma in the morning sun, while the large hall in the house turns to the shady fern garden with its high glass facade towards the north east. A green radiance fills the festive lobby space which stretches across two floors. The interior and exterior unite into an atmospheric whole and yet the sharp contrast between the dark slate gray of the inside tile covering and the light gray concrete of the outside coverings forms a transparency which consciously prevents the disappearing of transitions.

"During the summer I endeavor to escape the heat of the midday sun, preferably in the fern garden where there's always a slight breeze. Here, I am reminded of a secret place in the forest."

'The outside space must be a sensual place.'

Udo Weilacher

---

[1] All quotes in single marks are taken from a conversation with Dieter Kienast during summer 1995.
[1] All quotes in double marks are taken from a conversation with the L. family during spring 1996.

Der dunkle Wasserspiegel reicht haarscharf unter die Oberkante
des rostroten bis schwärzlichen Rohstahls, er wirkt wie ein rahmenloser Spiegel im
Garten und erfaßt seismographisch die Lebendigkeit seiner Umgebung ...

The mirroring surface of the dark water reaches just up to the upper edge of
the rusty red to black raw steel and seems to be a frameless mirror in the garden,
seismographically taking in the liveliness of its surroundings ....

Zwischen Tradition und Innovation

Ökologie ist nicht nur ein vielzitiertes gesellschaftliches Schlagwort, sie ist auch eine wichtige Grundlage unserer Arbeit. Das Verständnis ökologischer Wirkungsweisen und deren Umsetzung gehört zur Grundlage verantwortungsvollen Bauens in unserer Zeit. Bei der Durchsicht unserer Projekte mag dies überraschen, weil man gewohnt ist, Ökologie mit bestimmten Eigenschaften oder Bildern gleichzusetzen: das Feuchtbiotop, die Ruderalvegetation, die artenreiche Blumenwiese, die Feldhecke, das Waldstück, den Wintergarten haben wir im Kopf und denken an Gesundes, Natürliches, vom Menschen wenig Beeinflußtes, Nachhaltiges. Dabei bedeutet Ökologie nur «die Lehre von den Beziehungen der Lebewesen zu ihrer Umwelt». Ökologisch ist demnach die Blumenwiese, aber auch die zunehmende Verbreitung der Malaria. Loslösen von den vordergründigen Bildern und nach der Funktionsweise, nach der Materialität, dem Herstellungsaufwand, der Nachhaltigkeit und Reziklierbarkeit fragen. Überrascht stellen wir dann vielleicht fest, daß das Alternativenergiehaus ökologisch schlechtere Werte zeigt als das einfache Backsteinhaus, daß das natürlich erscheinende Feuchtbiotop nur dank einer kaum entsorgbaren PVC-Folie funktioniert. Wir setzen auf ein vertieftes, hintergründiges Ökologiever-

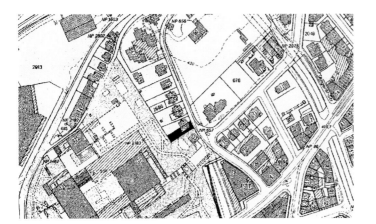

Between Tradition and Innovation

Ecology is not only a much quoted social slogan. It has also become an important basis for our work. Understanding ecological effects and realizing them is part of the basis for a responsible architecture in our days. This may come as a surprise when viewing our projects because we are accustomed to associating ecology with very specific characteristics or images: the damp biotope, the ruderal vegetation, the rich, flowering meadow, the field hedge, the forest, the winter garden. All these things are on our minds and we think of something healthy, natural, little influenced by man and enduring. Yet, all that ecology means is "the teaching of the relationships of the living beings with their environment". According to this, the flowering meadow is as ecological, as is the increasing spread of Malaria. One has to distance oneself from the obvious images and ask about the function, the material, the effort of production, the lifetime and the recyclability. Then we may be surprised to find that the alternative energy house has a worse ecological value than the simple brick house, that the seemingly natural damp biotope functions only due to an almost non-recyclable PVC foil. We count on a deeper knowledge of understanding of ecology and, at the same time, emphasize that not only ecology, but also the design and the use are equivalent parameters in our gardens.

The quarter is distinguished by the grid-like development dating back to the 'Gründerzeit' (years of rapid industrial expansion in Germany) and the single villas with larger gardens. Our property is located on a street with row houses from the turn of the century. The 11 m wide and 40 m long garden space shows, like the adjoining properties, a unified zoning pattern: walkway, wall and forecourt which is connected by a small passageway with the garden.

The building, which was successfully converted by the architects Romero & Schaefle, and the school yard with a beautiful old tree population on the south side become the starting point for the new garden concept. The four space-defining borders are designed differently. The forecourt is

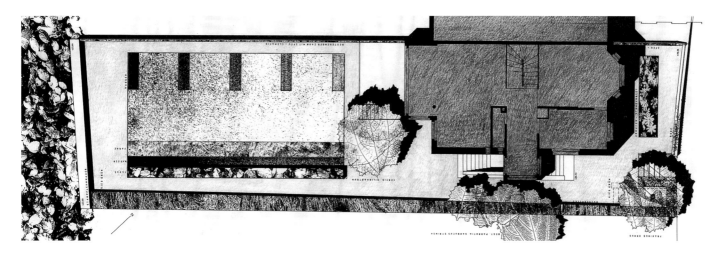

ständnis und betonen gleichzeitig, daß nicht nur Ökologie, sondern auch die Gestalt und der Gebrauch gleichberechtigte Parameter unserer Gärten sind.

Das Stadtviertel wird durch die rasterartige Gründerzeitbebauung und einzelnen Villen mit größeren Gärten geprägt. Unser Grundstück liegt an einer Straße mit zusammengebauten Wohnhäusern aus der Jahrhundertwende. Der 11 Meter schmale und 40 Meter lange Gartenraum zeigt ebenso wie die angrenzenden Grundstücke ein einheitliches Zonierungsmuster: Gehsteig, Mauer und Vorgarten, der mit einen schmalen Durchgang mit dem Wohngarten verbunden ist.

Das Gebäude, von den Architekten Romero & Schaefle gekonnt umgebaut, und der südlich angrenzende Schulhausfreiraum mit schönem alten Baumbestand wird zum Ausgangspunkt der neuen Gartenkonzeption. Die vier raumdefinierenden Grenzen werden unterschiedlich ausgebildet. Der Vorgarten wird mit einem einfachen Metallzaun gefaßt. Er orientiert sich zur Straße und ist voll einsehbar. Der Vorgarten ist gleichermaßen Empfangsraum, Distanzhalter und ‹Visitenkarte› seiner Bewohner. Die 40 Meter lange, sich verdickende Buchenhecke auf der Ostseite, betont die Länge des Gartens und gibt den Ausblick in den anliegenden Schulgarten frei. Gegenüber wird der alte Zaun berankt und somit die Ungleichseitigkeit des Wohngartens verdeutlicht. Die südseitige Grenze steht,

framed with a simple metal fence. It is oriented towards the street and is completely open to view. The forecourt is a reception area and, at the same time, creates a certain distance. It is, so to speak, the "business card" of the occupants. The 40 m long beech hedge on the east side enhances the length of the garden and reveals a view of the adjoining school garden. On the opposite side, the old fence is covered with climbing plants and the unevenness of the garden is thus made clear. The southern border, seen from the living room and terrace, is a view of central importance and represents the omnipresent terminating image with 20 m high beeches and yews, seemingly standing on the base of a new pressed loam wall of 2.50 m height.

The loam wall is an archaic building procedure which can be realized in our latitude, as well. It challenges the tradesmen to execute this kind of work once again. The 60 cm thick wall is framed like a concrete wall. The humus and slightly clayey earth material is filled into the frame in layers and then stomped down. The wall is then covered with a rusting steel plate to prevent water from draining into it. The layers of soil remain visible in their various shades of brown. The wall shows a 'lively' mutable picture which changes in color and structure depending on the time of day and year. It has thus become the bearer of the image of the ordinarily hidden earth and contrasts strikingly with the differing greens of the plants and the gravel.

Projektplan 1994
Grundriß
Original 1:50, 40 x 90 cm;
Tusche, Folie, Farbstift
auf Plandruck weiß

Project plan 1994
ground plan
Original 1:50, 40 x 90 cm;
ink, foil, colored pencil
on white plan print

von Wohnzimmer und Terrasse aus betrachtet, im direkten Blickfeld und stellt das omnipräsente Abschlußbild mit 20 Meter hohen Buchen und vorgelagerten Eiben dar, das scheinbar auf dem Sockel einer neuen, 2.50 Meter hohen Stampflehmmauer steht.

Die Stampflehmmauer ist ein archaisches, auch in unseren Breitengraden mögliches Bauverfahren, bei dem die handwerkliche Umsetzung neu erprobt werden muß. Die 60 cm dicke Mauer wird wie eine Betonmauer geschalt. Darin wird das vor Ort vorhandene, humose und etwas lehmhaltige Erdmaterial schichtweise eingebracht und festgestampft. Die Mauerabdeckung erfolgt mit einer rostenden Stahlplatte, die das Einsickern des Wassers verhindert. Die Erdschichten bleiben in ihren differenten Brauntönen sichtbar. Die Mauer zeigt ein ‹lebendig› wechselndes Bild, das sich in Tages- und Jahresverlauf, in Farbe und Struktur verändert. Sie ist damit zum Bildträger der normalerweise verborgenen Erde geworden und kontrastiert auffällig das unterschiedliche Grün der Pflanzen und des grünen Gartenkieses.

Farbigen Teppichen gleich, im Kies eingefügt, sind im Vorgarten ein Kräuterbeet und im Wohngarten ein Rasenbeet plaziert. Die Begrenzung des Rasenbeetes erfolgt auf der Längsseite mit einer hohen Eibenhecke, dem Wasserbecken und Farnstreifen. Diese spielen mit der ambivalenten Grundkonzeption des asymmetrischen Gartens. Wegeinfassungen und das Wasserbecken sind aus unbehandeltem Stahl angefertigt, der Rost ist selbstverständlicher Teil der Elemente, die Patina ansetzen und darüber hinaus dem Wasser einen schönen Farbton beigeben. An markanten Stellen des Vor- und Wohngartens betonen Cercidiphyllum japonicum und Cornus controversa die Raumhaltigkeit des Gartens und werden mit Laub, Blüte und Duft sinnlich erfahrbar.

Der kleine Garten für die Familie K. ist der Versuch, das Gefäß eines stimmungsvollen Gartens zu schaffen, dessen Weiterentwicklung oder Füllung sie selber übernehmen wollen und müssen, aber auch die Fortschreibung der Gartentypologie des anliegenden Stadtviertels.

Dieter Kienast

Similar to colored carpets imbedded in the gravel, an herb bed is placed in the forecourt and a lawn bed in the garden. The lawn bed is framed on its longitudinal side by a tall yew hedge, the water basin and strips of fern. They play with the ambivalent basic conception of the asymmetrical garden. The edges of the pathways and the water basin are trimmed with raw steel, the rust is a self-understood part of the elements which create a patina and, furthermore, provide the water with a nice hue. The spaciousness of the garden is marked in important places of the forecourt and garden by Cercidiphyllum japonicum and Cornus controversa and can be sensually experienced through their foliage, blossoms and scent.

The small garden for the K. family is an attempt to create a vessel for the creation of an atmospheric garden whose further development or filling-in, but also the continuation of the garden typology of the adjoining quarter, is and has to be effected by the family itself.

Dieter Kienast

Die südseitige Grenze steht, von Wohnzimmer und Terrasse aus betrachtet, im direkten Blickfeld und stellt das omnipräsente Abschlußbild mit 20 Meter hohen Buchen und vorgelagerten Eiben dar...

The southern border, seen from the living room and terrace, is a view of central importance and represents the omnipresent terminating image with 20 m high beeches and yews ...

Die Erdschichten bleiben in ihren differenten Brauntönen sichtbar. Die Mauer zeigt ein ‹lebendig› wechselndes Bild, das sich in Tages- und Jahresverlauf, in Farbe und Struktur verändert. Sie ist damit zum Bildträger der normalerweise verborgenen Erde geworden ...

The layers of soil remain visible in their various shades of brown. The wall shows a 'lively' mutable picture which changes in color and structure depending on the time of day and year. It has thus become the bearer of the image of the ordinarily hidden earth ...

Mimesis. Ein botanischer Garten

Wie sieht der Garten für Botaniker aus?

    Moos Lehm Solitärbienen
    Taschentuchbaum Sand Libellen Binsen Kies
    Igel Spritzgurke Erde Schmetterlinge

Wie formt man diese Gedanken zu einem Garten?

Haus und Garten liegen in einem Reihenhausviertel am Greifensee. Vom Wohnen in einer reizvollen Landschaft zur Arbeit in der Stadt, pendeln fast alle hier. Zwischen diesen Welten ist die Frage nach Zentrum und Rand müßig. Vor diesem Hintergrund ist die lange und intensive inhaltliche Auseinandersetzung mit der Bauherrschaft, von der ersten Skizze bis zum Bau des neuen Gartens, zu verstehen.

    Ist der neue Garten ein erweitertes Forschungsfeld der täglichen Arbeit? Eine Miniaturisierung der Landschaft, ein Naturmodell?

    An der Längsseite des Gartens bildet eine lange Stampflehmmauer aus dem anstehenden Boden eine räumliche Grenze. Verwirrend ist, daß die Mauer nicht an der Grenze steht und auch Einblick in den dahinterliegenden Garten zuläßt. Innen und Außen ist damit nicht eine Frage des

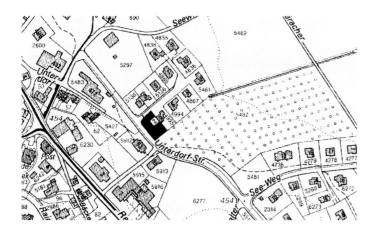

Mimesis. A Botanical Garden

What does the garden look like to botanists?

    Moss, loam, solitary bees, handkerchief tree,
    sand, dragon-flies, rushes, gravel, hedgehogs,
    cucumber, earth, butterflies

How can these thoughts be formed into a garden?

The house and garden are located in a neighborhood of row houses at Lake Greifen. Almost everyone commutes between life in an interesting landscape and work in the city. Between these worlds the question about center and periphery is superfluous. The long and intensive contextual discussion with the clients, from the first sketch to the realization of the new garden, must be understood given this background.

    Is the new garden an expanded field for researching daily toil? Is it a miniature of the landscape or a natural model?

    On the longitudinal side of the garden, a long pressed loam wall rising from the soil forms a spatial border. What is confusing is that the wall is not situated on the border and even allows a view into the garden behind it. Thus, the inside and outside is not a question of location. The fruit trees and ornate trees of the neighboring gardens limit the space.

    Prefabricated concrete tiles in an amorphous shape reach out into the garden from the sitting area near the house. The tiles, some of them over seven meters long, refuse the smallness of this suburban place in a way that is similar to the long wall.

    Outside the living room, seven geometrically precise rectangular stone panels rise up from the earth. At a distance of two centimeters, glass planes are fixed in front of each one. In time, these glass planes will be imprinted with various scientific drawings of insects who inhabit the tuff. In the 16th century, scholars developed an enthusiasm for

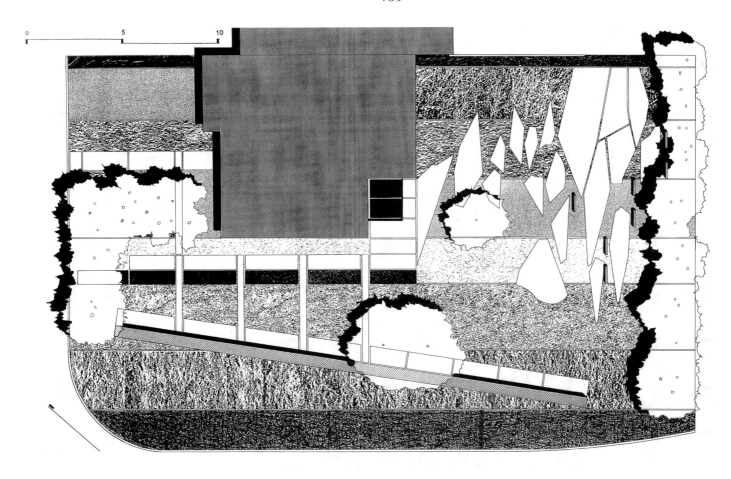

Standorts. Vielmehr begrenzen Obst- und Zierbäume der Nachbargärten den Raum.

Vorfabrizierte Betonplatten in amorpher Form greifen vom Sitzplatz am Haus in den Garten. Die teils über sieben Meter langen Platten sperren sich ähnlich wie die lange Mauer gegen die Kleinteiligkeit dieses suburbanen Ortes.

Vor dem Wohnzimmer ragen sieben geometrisch präzise, rechteckige Steinplatten aus der Erde. In einem Abstand von zwei Zentimetern ist jeweils eine Glasplatte davor fixiert. Im Lauf der Jahre werden diese Glasplatten mit unterschiedlichen wissenschaftlichen Zeichnungen von Insekten, die im Tuffstein mit der Zeit ihre Lebensstätte finden, bedruckt. Im 16. Jahrhundert entwickelten die Gelehrten eine Leidenschaft im Sammeln und Systemati-

Projektplan 2. Entwurf 1995
Grundriß
Original 1:50, 46 x 95 cm; Tusche, Folie, Kreide auf Großxerox weiß

Project plan, 2nd design 1995
Ground plan
Original 1:50, 46 x 95 cm; ink, foil, crayon on white Xerox copy

Ansicht Tuffsteinplatte
und bedrucktes Glas

Tuff stone panel and
'printed' glass

sieren von Pflanzen und Tieren. Conrad Gessners Werke, in Zürich entstanden, machten die Schweiz zu einem Zentrum der systematischen Naturkunde. Die flämischen Maler jener Zeit bevölkerten den Vordergrund ihrer Bilder mit Muscheln, Schnecken, Reptilien und Insekten, den Hintergrund mit pflanzlichen Elementen, Früchten, Gemüsen und Ästen. Neben der Entdeckungs- und Sammelleidenschaft in überbordender Fülle, Farbenpracht und Frische ist der bald zu erwartende Abbau- und Verfallsprozeß Inhalt des gleichen Bildes.

Lehm, Sand, Kies, Erde bedecken streifenförmig den Gartenboden. Präzise begrenzt erscheinen sie durch die unterschiedliche Textur wie Versuchsflächen für Pflanzenanbau. Zwischen Haus und Lehmmauer sind schmale Wasserbehälter auf den Sandboden aufgelegt. Die ursprüngliche Großvegetation wie die Wildhecke an der Südgrenze, die Schlehe vor dem Sitzplatz und die Bäume vor dem Hauseingang sind Teil des neuen Gartens.

Der Garten liegt in einem Landschaftsschutzgebiet. Fremdländische Pflanzen dürfen demnach nicht gepflanzt werden. Trotzdem wachsen in den Nachbargärten Scheinzypresse, Blautanne und Forsythie vorzüglich. Aber auch in diesem Garten ist das Fremde durchaus heimisch. Dem kundigen Auge bleibt nicht verborgen, daß zwischen Hauhechel, wilder Möhre und Geißblatt auch Psoralea bituminosa, Gynandriris sisyrinchium und Tetragonolobus purpureus gedeihen. Von über siebenhundert Pflanzen sind etwa ein Drittel fremdländisch. Auf Exkursionen gesammelte Pflanzen werden in das ihren spezifischen Ansprüchen entsprechende Substrat gepflanzt oder gesät. Die Bepflanzung des Gartens ist damit nicht nach planerischen Vorgaben angelegt, sondern das Resultat der täglichen Arbeit der Bewohner.

collecting and categorizing plants and animals. Conrad Gessner's works, which were created in Zurich, made Switzerland a center of the systematic study of natural science. The Flemish painters of those days put shells, snails, reptiles and insects into the foreground of their paintings, and plants, fruits, vegetables and branches into the background. Aside from the passion for discovery and collecting in an overwhelming wealth, glorious colors and freshness, the process of decay – which is to be expected – is just as much an element of these same paintings as the former.

Clay, sand, gravel and earth cover the garden grounds in stripes. Precisely framed and with different textures, they appear to be experimental fields for planting. Between the house and the loam wall, small water containers are laid onto the sand. The original large vegetation, such as the wild hedge at the southern border, the sloe in front of the sitting area and the trees in front of the house entrance are all part of the new garden.

The garden is located in a landscape preserve. As a result, exotic plants may not be planted, despite the fact that, in the neighboring gardens, false cypresses, blue fir and forsythia grow very well. But in this garden, too, the non-native is right at home. The knowledgeable eye easily detects that between the Ononis, wild carrots and honeysuckle, one can also find Psoralea bituminosa, Gynandriris sisyrinchium and Tetragonolobus purpureus. About one third of the seven hundred plants are from foreign countries. Plants collected on excursions are planted or sowed into the substrate appropriate to their specific needs. The plantings in the garden are, therefore, not a result of a planned layout, but of the daily work by its inhabitants.

Vorfabrizierte Betonplatten in amorpher Form greifen vom Sitzplatz
am Haus in den Garten. Die teils über sieben Meter langen Platten sperren sich ...
gegen die Kleinteiligkeit dieses suburbanen Ortes ...

Prefabricated concrete tiles in an amorphous shape reach out into
the garden from the sitting area near the house. The tiles, some of them
over seven meters long, refuse the smallness of this suburban place ...

... Substrat gepflanzt oder gesät. Die Bepflanzung des Gartens ist damit nicht nach planerischen Vorgaben angelegt, sondern das Resultat der täglichen Arbeit der Bewohner.

... planted or sowed into the substrate. The plantings in the garden are, therefore, not a result of a planned layout, but of the daily work by its inhabitants.

An der Längsseite des Gartens bildet eine lange Stampflehmmauer aus
dem anstehenden Boden eine räumliche Grenze. Verwirrend ist,
daß die Mauer nicht an der Grenze steht und auch Einblick in den dahinterliegenden Garten zuläßt. Innen und Außen ...

On the longitudinal side of the garden, a long pressed loam wall
rising from the soil forms a spatial border. What is confusing
is that the wall is not situated on the border and even allows a view
into the garden behind it. Inside and outside ...

Willkür und Kontext. Ein Lindengarten

Eine Kleinstadt. Dem anonymen Wohnblock gegenüber ein kleinbäuerliches Anwesen, dazwischen Einfamilienhäuser. Ein dreigeschossiger Gewerbebau hebt sich wohltuend ab von diesem Konglomerat unbestimmter Formen und räumlichen Zuordnungen. Jeder Versuch, eine städtebauliche Ordnung mit Neubauten oder der Gestaltung des Außenraumes zu erreichen, muß scheitern.

Die Frage, wieweit der Garten eine Erweiterung des Hauses ist, stellt sich hier nicht. Die Beziehung ‹Haus – Garten› gibt es nicht, da das Erdgeschoß ungenutzt bleibt, das Obergeschoß in eine Wohnung und das Dachgeschoß zu einem Arbeitsraum umgebaut wird.

Wegen des komplexen Grundstückszuschnittes ergeben sich zwei völlig unterschiedliche Gartenräume. Der direkt an das Haus stoßende Raum an der Längsseite des Baukörpers mit dem seitlichen Eingang und der quer an der Stirnseite weit über das Haus laufende eigentliche schmale Gartenraum. Diese Abwicklung und Raumbezüge vereinnahmen die heterogene Siedlungsstruktur. An dem kleinen Vorplatz stehen drei geschnittene Linden an der Straße in einer Reihe. Der Nachbargarten wird von zwei imposanten Linden dominiert.

Diese ausgewählten Zufälligkeiten sind die Essenz des neuen Gartenkonzepts.

An der Längsseite begrenzt eine unarmierte, dicke Stampfbetonmauer den Raum zum Nachbarn. Den Abschluß dieses Hofraumes bildet die imposante Linde im Nachbargarten. Lange Wassergefäße nehmen an der Stirnseite des Gebäudes das Regenwasser von Platz und Dach auf. Das erste Wasserbecken ist mit Seerosen bepflanzt, über ein mit Binsen bepflanztes Becken gelangt das Wasser in ein Sandbecken, wo es versickert. Die Aquakulturen dienen also nicht industriellen Reinigungsprozessen, wie dies bei der Textilveredlung, der ursprünglichen Nutzung des Gebäudes, üblich war. Das Wasser selbst durchläuft einen Reinigungsprozess, bevor es in den Naturkreislauf zurückgelangt.

Arbitrariness and Context. A Lime Tree Garden

A small town. Opposite from the new housing block lies a small farm estate, and between them, single-family-homes. A three-story industrial building stands out nicely from this conglomerate of undefined forms and spatial arrangements. Every attempt to attain an urban order with new buildings or the design of the outside space is destined to fail.

The question, in so far as the garden is an extension of the house, does not occur in this case. The relationship 'house – garden' does not exist since the first floor remains unused, the second floor is converted into an apartment and the attic into a work space.

Due to the complex layout of the property, two entirely different garden spaces come into being. The space on the longitudinal side of the building volume goes directly up to the house with an entrance on its side, and the garden space running laterally along the front side reaches far beyond the house and is rather narrow. This arrangement and spatial relationship claims the heterogeneous structure of the development. Along the street of the small forecourt three trimmed lime trees are standing in a row. The neighboring garden is dominated by two impressive lime trees. These selected coincidences are the essence of the new garden concept.

A thick pressed loam wall limits the space on the longitudinal side towards the neighbor. The termination of this yard is formed by the impressive lime tree in the neighboring garden. Long water containers receive the rain water from the square and roof on the front side of the building. The first water basin is planted with water lilies. The water then goes through a basin planted with rushes and reaches a sand basin where it seeps away. The aqua cultures are not designed for industrial cleansing procedures as they were when the building was being used for its original purpose – textile processing. The water itself runs through a cleansing process before reentering the natural cycle.

Behind the new garage stands a lime tree hedge which detaches from the border at the transition point into the

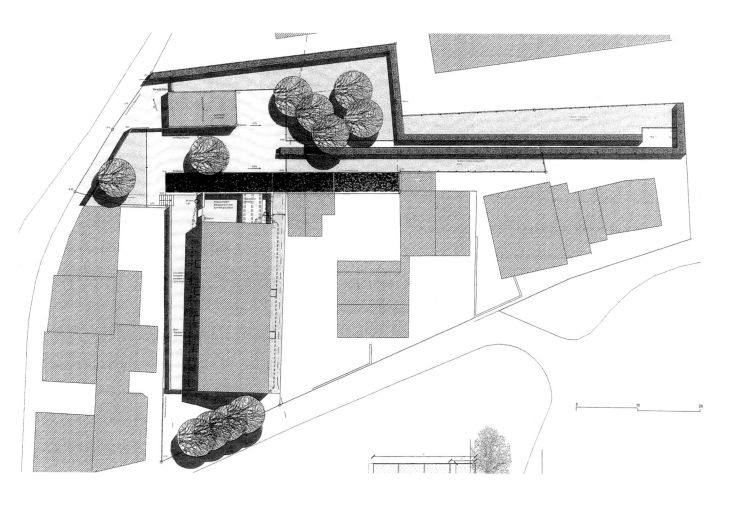

Projektplan 1996
Grundriß
CAD-Plan 1:100, 60 x 105 cm

Project plan 1996
Ground plan
CAD-plan 1:100, 60 x 105 cm

Hinter der neugebauten Garage steht eine Lindenhecke, die sich beim Übergang in den schmalen Gartenraum von der Grenze ablöst. Das verwirrende räumliche Vorspringen der Hecke wird bei einem Spaziergang durch den Garten nicht aufgelöst. In dieser eintönigen Vielfalt von Resträumen fassen die Linden zwar großzügige Gartenräume, bilden zugleich aber auch neue kleinteilige. Teilweise werden diese kleinteiligen Gartenräume, wie bis anhin, von den Nachbarn als Gemüsegarten genutzt. Unter der Lindenhecke begleitet uns im Mai der Duft von Maiglöckchen. Waldstauden wachsen im Hain aus frei wachsenden Linden.

Das unverkennbare Lindengrün im Frühjahr im Kontrast zu der schwarzen Rinde, der weitstreifende Duft der Blüten im Sommer, das fahle Gelb der Blätter im Herbst und die langhaftenden Früchte im Winter prägen diesen Garten.

Die Linden in unterschiedlichen Wuchsformen und die Anordnung der Gartenräume beziehen sich auf das vorhandene Vertraute. Bei einem Spaziergang durch den Garten ist das Konglomerat von Alt und Neu spürbar. Erinnerungen werden geweckt an eine Gartentradition, die man an diesem Ort nicht erwartet.

narrow garden space. The confusing spatial shift of the hedge is not resolved when walking through the garden. In this monotonous multitude of remaining spaces the lime trees embrace generous garden spaces; however, at the same time, they also form new smaller ones. Some of these garden spaces continue to be used by the neighbors as vegetable gardens as they were in the past. In May, the scent of lilies of the valley accompanies us beneath the lime tree hedge. Forest shrubs are spread throughout the grove with its freely growing lime trees.

The unmistakable green of the limes in spring as a contrast to the black bark, the far reaching scent of the blossoms in summer, the pale yellow of the leaves in fall and the long-lasting fruit in winter distinguish this garden.

The lime trees in different forms and the arrangement of the garden spaces refer to the existing, the familiar. When walking through the garden, the conglomerate of old and new is perceivable. Memories of a garden tradition arise which one does not expect in this location.

Die Linden in unterschiedlichen Wuchsformen und die Anordnung der Gartenräume beziehen sich auf das vorhandene Vertraute. Bei einem Spaziergang durch den Garten ist das Konglomerat von Alt und Neu spürbar.

The lime trees in different forms and the arrangement of the garden spaces refer to the existing, the familiar. When walking through the garden, the conglomerate of old and new is perceivable.

... über ein mit Binsen bepflanztes Becken gelangt das Wasser in ein Sandbecken, wo es versickert. Die Aquakulturen dienen also nicht industriellen Reinigungsprozessen ...

The water then goes through a basin planted with rushes and reaches a sand basin where it seeps away. The aqua cultures are not designed for industrial cleansing procedures...

... schmale Gartenraum. Diese Abwicklung und Raumbezüge
vereinnahmen die heterogene Siedlungsstruktur.

The garden space is rather narrow. This arrangement and spatial relationship claims the heterogeneous structure of the development.

Neue Gärten zum alten Schloß

Die genuine Eigenschaft des Gartens ist seine – durch das Pflanzenwachstum bedingte – permanente Veränderung, die letztlich durch noch so intensive Pflege nicht aufgehalten werden kann. Darin begründen sich die bis in die jüngste Zeit anhaltenden Zweifel über den Wert des Kulturgutes Garten und damit auch über die Notwendigkeit seines Schutzes vor der Zerstörung. Das Nachdenken über den Umgang mit unserem historischen Erbe beschränkte sich deshalb lange Zeit auf die Bauten, während die Gärten erst in den 60er und 70er Jahren zum Gegenstand fundierter wissenschaftlicher Untersuchungen geworden sind. In der Gartendenkmalpflege hat die Denkmalpflege eine Diversifikation gefunden, deren Grundsätze 1981 in der Charta von Florenz festgelegt und seither in zahllosen Publikationen verfeinert diskutiert werden. Es liegt im Trend der Zeit, daß das Alte in der Fachdiziplin und der Gesellschaft eine zunehmende Wertschätzung erfährt. So hat sich die Gartendenkmalpflege zumindest in den deutschsprachigen Ländern relativ rasch emanzipiert und verteidigt selbstbewußt das neu gewonnene Terrain. Der sorgsame Umgang mit vorhandenen Gärten ist zweifelsohne wichtig. Trotzdem stimmen zwei Aspekte in der Praxis nachdenklich:

Trotz der, in der Fachliteratur eindeutig ablehnenden Haltung gegenüber Rekonstruktionen beobachten wir gerade in jüngster Zeit eine Vielzahl von Rekonstruktionen oder, noch problematischer, historisierende Neuschöpfungen. Zum Zweiten stellen wir eine große Skepsis gegenüber dem Weiterbauen, dem Neubauen in alten Gärten fest. Damit wird aber gerade verhindert, was die moderne Denkmalpflege propagiert: nicht ein bestimmter Zustand ist erhaltenswert, sondern die unterschiedlichen Sedimentationen der Geschichte. Dies schließt bewußt auch neueste Bauteile mit ein unter der Bedingung, daß das Neue als solches erkennbar bleibt. Ist dies bei den Bauten durch die Verwendung aktueller Baumaterialien und entsprechender Anwendung signifikant herstellbar, so stellt sich im Garten

New Gardens for the Old Castle

Because of the plant growth, which can not be stopped no matter how intensive the care may be, one genuine characteristic of the garden is its permanent transformation. This is a basis for doubts about the value of the cultural good of the garden and the necessity of its protection from destruction. Therefore, thoughts about the handling of our historic heritage were for a long time limited to buildings, whereas gardens became the object of scientific research only in the '60s and '70s. Monumental preservation has found a diversification in the garden preservation whose principles were set in 1981 by the charter of Florence and have been discussed in many publications ever since. It is the trend of our times for the traditional to experience increased attention and appreciation in special disciplines and society as a whole. Thus, garden preservation has emancipated rather quickly, at least in the German speaking countries, and it self-consciously defends its newly found territory. The careful handling of existing gardens is, without any doubt, important. Still, two aspects in practice make you think:

Despite what is clearly an attitude of refusal in specialized literature towards reconstruction, we can observe, es-

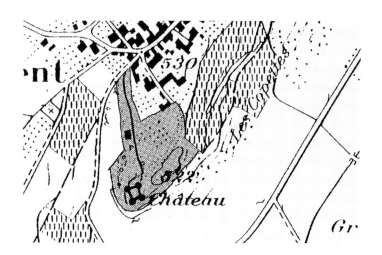

185

Projektplan 1995
Grundriß
Original 1:250, 87 x 102 cm;
Tusche, Folie
auf Plandruck weiß

Project plan 1995
Ground plan
Original 1:250, 87 x 102 cm;
ink, foil on
white plan print

beim wichtigsten Element ‹Pflanze› die Frage nach der Ablesbarkeit in höchster Brisanz: der Buchs, die Buche, der Holunder haben auch heute das gleiche Aussehen wie vor 300 Jahren. Die Verwendung ‹moderner› Baumaterialien ist zwar möglich, erscheint im Hinblick auf das Ensemble jedoch meist nur Notbehelf zu sein. Neues Bauen in alten Gärten wird deshalb immer eine heikle Gratwanderung zwischen dem angestrengten ‹Sichtbarmachen› des neuen Eingriffes, dem selbstbewußten Weiterbauen und der Rekonstruktion sein. Entscheidend scheint, daß in Raumkonzeption, Material, Vegetation für veränderte Nutzungsansprüche und Rahmenbedingungen zeitgemäße Lösungen entwickelt werden, die im Dialog oder vielleicht auch in Opposition zur historischen Substanz stehen.

Mitte des 13. Jahrhunderts wurde mit dem Bau des Schlosses durch Henri von Ch. begonnen. Eine wehrhafte Burg mit vier Türmen entstand in der Waadt, markant am Rand des Hochplateaus gelegen, mit beeindruckender Sicht ins Tal nach Süden und Osten. 1478–1505 erfolgte unter dem Bauherrn Erzherzog Maximilian der Umbau zum Schloß, so wie es heute noch im wesentlichen besteht. Dendrochronologische Untersuchungen belegen, daß alle Deckenbalken vom Ende des 15. Jahrhunderts stammen. Das Château de Ch. und die dazugehörigen Ländereien haben im Verlauf der Geschichte viele wechselnde Eigentümer erlebt, bis es 1989 von den jetzigen Besitzern erworben wurde. Vielleicht sind die vielen Handänderungen verantwortlich dafür, daß relativ wenig Pläne und Schriften vom Schloß vorhanden sind. Ein Stich aus dem 18. Jahrhundert zeigt, daß der Schloßhügel vollständig mit Weinterrassen bedeckt war, während im flacheren Teil nordöstlich des Schlosses Obstbäume und Gemüsebeete sichtbar sind.

Von dieser intensiven Landwirtschaftsnutzung sind bis heute wichtige Teile geblieben. Der Weinanbau am Schloßosthang ist großflächig erhalten, der jetzt mit Mauern eingefriedete Schloßpark wird zur Hälfte beweidet. In den Steilhängen der Süd- und Westseite stockt ein 100 jähriger Wald, während auf der Ostterrasse eine ca. 150 Jahre alte Lindenallee vom Schloßeingang zu einem zugewachsenen Aussichtsplatz führt. Inmitten des Wieslandes

pecially in recent times, an abundance of reconstruction activity. Or – and this may be even more problematic – new creations from a reemerging history. Secondly, we can perceive a marked skepticism towards the extension – new building in old gardens. This, however, prevents exactly what modern preservationism propagates: it's not a specific condition that is worth preserving, but rather the various sedimental layers of history. This consciously includes the newest building sections under the premise that the new can be recognized as such. Whereas, in the case of buildings this can, to a high degree, be attained by using current materials and an appropriate application, in the case of a garden and its most important element, the plant, the question of readability becomes highly incendiary: box, beech or elder still have the same appearance as they had 300 years ago. The use of 'modern' building materials is possible; however, with respect to the ensemble it seems to be just an expedient in most cases. Therefore, new construction in old gardens always becomes a tricky act of balance between the goal of making the new operation 'visible' and the self-confident continuation of the building and reconstruction. What seems to be decisive is that, when it comes to the spatial concept – material, vegetation, changed utilization expectations and framework conditions – new contemporary solutions are developed which stand in a dialogue or, perhaps, in opposition with the historic substance.

In the middle of the 13th century the construction of the castle was started by Henri of Ch. A weir-like castle with four towers was created in the Waadt, strikingly situated at the edge of the high plateau with an impressive view of the valley towards the south and east. From 1478 to 1505 the archduke Maximilian had the castle converted to what, essentially, can be seen today. Dendrochronological research proves that all ceiling rafters date back to the end of the 15th century. The 'Château de Ch.' and the estates have seen many changes of owners in the course of history until it was bought in 1989 by its current owners. Perhaps the many changes of hands is responsible for the existence of relatively few plans and historical writings of the castle. An 18th century etching shows that the castle

liegt ein – wohl im letzten Jahrhundert angelegter – Hofgarten mit einem kleinen, verfallenen Gewächshaus. Lindenallee, Hofgarten und Zedern im Wald zeigen, daß im letzten Jahrhundert die ersten Anstrengungen zur Anlage eines Parkes um das Schloß herum unternommen worden sind. Die neu geplanten Interventionen stellen die Weiterführung der Gestaltung des 19. Jahrhunderts dar. Dabei geht es um die Präzisierung bestehender Anlageteile, ohne die historische Substanz anzutasten, sowie um die Neuschaffung von Gartenteilen, die bisher landwirtschaftlich genutzt wurden.

Der Bereich der Vorfahrt und Ostterrasse ist im Verlauf der letzten hundert Jahre vor allem durch den Vegetationsbewuchs und Pflanzungen verunklärt worden. Im Schloßhof werden die vorhandenen Rasenkompartimente entlang der Wege mit Buchshecken gefaßt, der Hauptweg ist von Buchskegeln begleitet. Die Heckenbänder sind gegenüber den historischen Vorbildern vergleichbarer Anlagen überdimensioniert breit und gegen die Hofmauern offen gehalten. Der große Eingangsplatz wird seitlich durch breitgezogene Eibenkegel gefaßt. Dem Schloßeingang vorgelagert ist ein kleiner, tiefer gelegener Garten, der neu mit Rosen und Stauden bepflanzt ist.

Die Lindenalleeachse wird zur Landschaft geöffnet, der Weg wiederhergestellt und mit einem Wasserbecken abgeschlossen. Dieses wird von Eibenkugeln flankiert und endet auf dem Aussichtsplatz. Linkerhand führt eine Trep-

hill was entirely laid out as vineyard terraces, whereas, on the flatter part northeast of the castle grounds, fruit trees and vegetable beds are visible.

Important parts of this intensive agricultural utilization have been preserved up to this day. The viticulture on the eastern side of the castle hill still covers a large surface, and half of the castle park, which is now enclosed by walls, is used as pasture grounds. A century-old forest is situated on the steep slopes of the south and west sides, whereas, on the eastern terrace an approximately 150 year old alley of lime trees leads from the castle entrance to an overgrown outlook. In the midst of the pasture lies a garden court – probably laid out during the last century – with a small, dilapidated greenhouse. The lime tree alley, the garden court and the cedars in the forest reveal that, during the past century, the first efforts for laying out a park around the castle were undertaken.

The area of the access road and eastern terrace has become unclear during the past hundred years. This is due, above all, to the growth of the vegetation and new plantings. In the courtyard of the castle, the existing lawn sections are framed with box along the pathways, the main pathway is accompanied by box cones. Compared to the historic examples of similar complexes, the hedges are dimensionally too wide and they remain open towards the court walls. The large entrance area is framed laterally by trimmed yew cones. In front of the castle entrance there is a small garden on a lower level which has recently been planted with new roses and shrubbery.

The lime tree corridor axis is opened up towards the landscape and the pathway has been reestablished and terminated with a concrete water basin. The water basin is framed by yew balls and ends at the outlook. To its left, a staircase leads in to the 'secret garden'. A water basin that was covered up by soil and foliage was renovated and now forms the center of the secret garden. The existing mix of planted shrubbery and wild bushes is continued.

During the '60s, a new road with a direct access to the village was built into the terrain on the eastern side with quite unfavorable results. This street is the reason for a remodeling of the terrain of the adjoining pasture grounds,

Stich Beginn 18. Jahrhundert,
Ansicht von Süden

Etching, 18th century,
view from the south

pe in den ‹verborgenen Garten›. Ein unter Erde und Laub verdecktes Wasserbecken wurde instand gesetzt und bildet den Mittelpunkt des verborgenen Gartens. Die vorgefundene Durchmischung angepflanzter Sträucher und Stauden mit Wildwuchs wird fortgeschrieben.

Die nachfolgenden Gartenteile befinden sich zur Zeit in der weiteren Plandetaillierung. In den 60er Jahren wurde auf der Ostseite eine unschön ins Terrain gelegte Straße mit direktem Zugang zum Dorf gebaut. Die Straße ist Anlaß einer neuen Terrainmodellation des angrenzenden Weidelandes, das in einen landschaftlich gestalteten Garten mit Seerosenbecken übergeführt wird. Baumgruppen und Einzelbäume definieren den neuen Gartenteil, der mit einem Rundweg erschlossen wird.

Für den mauerbegrenzten Gemüsegartenhof wurde der Wunsch nach einem ‹historischen› Garten geäußert. Weil Geschichte bekanntlich nicht wiederholt werden kann, beabsichtigen wir im vorliegenden Projekt, durch Maßstabszerrung einen Prospekt aus einem Barockparterre zu zitieren, das bei flüchtiger Betrachtung vertraut wirkt, bei genauerem Hinsehen jedoch die Transformation verrät. Dezallier d'Argenville hat in seinem weitverbreiteten Buch ‹La théorie et la pratique du jardinage› eine bedeutendes Werk geschaffen, das wesentlich zur Verbreitung des barocken Gartenkonzeptes in ganz Europa beigetragen hat. Gut zweihundert Jahre später greifen auch wir auf eine seiner Vorlagen zurück und zeigen das stark vergrößerte Teilkompartiment eines Broderieparterre-Entwurfes. Der Vergrößerungsausschnitt ist so gewählt, daß die Axialität bzw. Symmetrie verweigert, wohl aber das prägnante Formenspiel erhalten bleibt. Der Rahmen mit den dreiseitigen Mauern und dem Metallzaun auf der Vorderseite soll erhalten bleiben.

So werden unterschiedlich alte Sedimentationen gestalterischer Eingriffe und des natürlichen Wachstums offengelegt und/oder weiterentwickelt. Wahrgenommen und gelesen werden die verschiedenen Gärten als neue, vielleicht hybride Parkanlage zum alten Schloß.

Dieter Kienast

which are transformed into a landscaped garden with a water-lily basin. Groups of trees and lone trees define the new part of the garden, which is accessed by a circular pathway.

The wish for a 'historic' garden was made for the vegetable garden yard enclosed by walls. With the present project, we intend to quote a prospect from a baroque parterre by distorting the scale because, as we all know, history can't be repeated. At first glance it will look familiar; however, it will reveal the transformation on a closer look. Dezallier d'Argenville has created an important oeuvre in his widely known book 'theory and practice of gardening' which contributed greatly to the spreading popularity of the baroque garden concept throughout Europe. Almost two hundred years later, we go back to one of his designs and show the strongly enlarged partial compartment of a broderie parterre design. The enlargement is chosen in order to reject the axis and symmetry while at the same time preserving the impressive play with the forms. The frame with the walls on three sides and the metal fence in the front remains.

In this way, the sedimental layers of different ages of design operations and natural growth are revealed and/or further developed. The different gardens are perceived and read as the new and perhaps hybrid park complex of the castle.

Dieter Kienast

Im Schloßhof werden die vorhandenen Rasenkompartimente entlang der Wege mit Buchshecken gefaßt, der Hauptweg ist von Buchskegeln begleitet.

In the courtyard of the castle, the existing lawn sections are framed
with box along the pathways, the main pathway is accompanied by box cones.

... Landschaft geöffnet, der Weg wieder hergestellt und mit einem Wasserbecken abgeschlossen. Dieses wird von Eibenkugeln flankiert und endet auf dem Aussichtsplatz.

... is opened up towards the landscape, the pathway has been reestablished and terminated with a water basin. The water basin is framed by yew balls and ends at the outlook.

Das Ausstellungsstück

Garten und Park als Thema von Ausstellungen haben Tradition. Von den anfänglichen Blumenschauen fand die Ausweitung zu großräumigen Dimensionen statt. Die Gartenschau als Messe des «Grünen Berufsstandes» nobilitierte zum Motor städtebaulicher Entwicklung und hat in Deutschland in der Nachkriegszeit ihre Hochblüte erlebt, um anschließend aus Mangel an innovativer Kraft in einen selbstgenügsamen Narzismus zu fallen.

Umso erfrischender wirkt daher die Konzeption des jährlich stattfindenden Gartenfestivals von Chaumont-sur-Loire in Frankreich, auf kleinstem Raum jeweils 30 Gärten von unterschiedlichsten Gestaltern zu zeigen. Hier wird die konzeptionelle Handschrift von Jean-Paul Pigeat, dem ehemaligen Ausstellungsmacher des Centre Pompidou deutlich. Von Jaques Wirz stammt der Gesamtplan des Ausstellungsgeländes mit den tulpenförmigen Heckengärten. Ein wahrhaftiger Blumenstrauß an Qualitätsvollem, Originellem, Absonderlichem, Banalem, Gebasteltem oder ökologisch Verbrämtem wird dem staunenden Besucher vorgeführt.

«La technique est-elle poétiquement correcte?» Das war das Jahresthema und somit auch der Inhalt unseres Beitrages 1996.

«nature n'existe pas»

Die Technik steht der Natur als Antipode gegenüber. Und wie bei jeder Gegensätzlichkeit ist trotzdem eine unmittelbare Beziehung zwischen den beiden Polen vorhanden. Überspitzt gesagt, wird die Natur erst in der Gegenüberstellung zur Technik in ihrer Wesenseigenschaft erkennbar. Umgekehrt erleben wir Technik im Spiegelbild der Natur am deutlichsten. Wenn Technik die «Gesamtheit aller Mittel ist, die Natur dem Menschen nutzbar zu machen», dann wird bereits hier der ambivalente Bedeutungsgehalt deutlich. Die aus der Natur entwickelte Technik findet im Garten eine anschauliche Metapher.

The Show Piece

The exhibition theme of garden and park has a tradition. Starting with the flower shows, the extension into large dimensions began to take place. The garden show, as the exhibition of the "green thumb profession", advanced to become the engine of urban development and had seen its heyday in the German post-war era – only to later fall into a self-contemptuous narcissism due to a lack of innovation.

More refreshing, therefore, is the effect of the concept of the annual garden festival in Chaumont-sur-Loire, France, to show, on the smallest space possible, 30 gardens by a gathering of the most diverse designers. Here, the conceptual signature of Jean-Paul Pigeat, the former exhibition manager of the Centre Pompidou, becomes clear. Jaques Wirz has designed the overall plan of the exhibition grounds with their tulip-shaped hedge gardens. A veritable bouquet of flowers made up of high quality, original, strange, banal, crafted or ecologically borderline objects is presented to the amazed visitor.

"Is technology poetically correct?" was the theme and, thus, also the content of our contribution in 1996.

"nature n'existe pas"

Technology is the antithesis of nature. And, as is the case with any contradiction, there still exists an immediate relationship between the two poles. Said in an exaggerated way, nature becomes visible in its being only when opposed to technology. Vice versa, we experience technology most clearly in the reflection of nature. If technology is "the entirety of all means to make nature useful to man", then the ambivalent content in meaning already becomes clear at that point. Technology developed from nature finds a vivid metaphor in the garden.

The analytical observation shows that the designed garden allows for ambiguous interpretations in its being. This ambiguity becomes the guiding motif of our garden in

Projektplan 1996
Grundriß, Schnitte, Perspektive
Original 1:100/1:20, 80 x 80 cm;
Tusche, Folie, Bleistift, Kreide
auf Großxerox weiß

Project plan 1996
Ground plan, sections, perspective
Original 1:100/1:20, 80 x 80 cm;
ink, foil, pencil, crayon on white
Xerox copy

Die analytische Betrachtung zeigt, daß der gestaltete Garten in seiner Wesensart vieldeutige Interpretationen zuläßt. Diese Vieldeutigkeit wird zum Leitmotiv unseres Gartens in Chaumont. Das zunächst eindeutig Erscheinende wird bei genauerer Betrachtung in Frage gestellt:

- Der vorhandene Heckenhof ist von außen als amorphe Form lesbar, während er sich beim Eintreten in die stärkste Geometrisierung eines quadratischen Raumes verwandelt.
- Der natürliche, unregelmäßige Erdboden außen wird durch den horizontal abgehobenen Holzboden ersetzt, der durch die hellblaue Farbe seine Materialnatürlichkeit verloren hat.
- Die rot in der Erde angekündigte «hommage à la nature» wird vom Schriftzug «nature n'existe pas» zunächst widerrufen, während die Buchstaben nachdrücklich die Existenz der Natur bestätigen.

Auf dem Coraystuhl sitzend, denken wir nach über den Charakter von Technik und Natur – oder wir lassen uns gehen und genießen die archaische Strenge des präzisen Gartenraumes, der gleichsam als Antipode paradiesischer Natur wirkt und erinnern uns, daß Gegensätzlichkeiten einander anziehen.

Kein Wort über Poesie.

Dieter Kienast

Chaumont. What seems to be clear at first is questioned upon closer inspection:

- The existing hedge yard can be read as an amorphous form from the outside while it turns into the strongest geometry of a square space upon entering.
- The natural irregular ground on the outside is replaced by the horizontally offset wooden floor which, due to the light blue color, has lost its natural appearance.
- The "hommage à la nature" announced in red letters in the earth is first taken back by the inscription "nature n'existe pas", whereas the letters emphatically confirm the existence of nature.

Sitting on the Coray chair, we think about the character of technology and nature – or we let ourselves go and enjoy the archaic strictness of the precise garden space which, at the same time, has the effect of an antipode of a paradise-like nature and we remember that opposites attract.

Not a word about poetry.

Dieter Kienast

Der natürliche, unregelmäßige Erdboden außen wird durch den horizontal abgehobenen Holzboden ersetzt, der durch die hellblaue Farbe seine Materialnatürlichkeit verloren hat.

The natural irregular ground on the outside is replaced by the horizontally offset wooden floor which, due to the light blue color, has lost its natural appearance.

Die rot in der Erde angekündigte «hommage à la nature» wird vom Schriftzug «nature n'existe pas» zunächst widerrufen, während die Buchstaben nachdrücklich die Existenz der Natur bestätigen.

The "hommage à la nature" announced in red letters in the earth is first taken back by the inscription "nature n'existe pas", whereas the letters emphatically confirm the existence of nature.

Gärten in Realisierung

Gardens in Progress

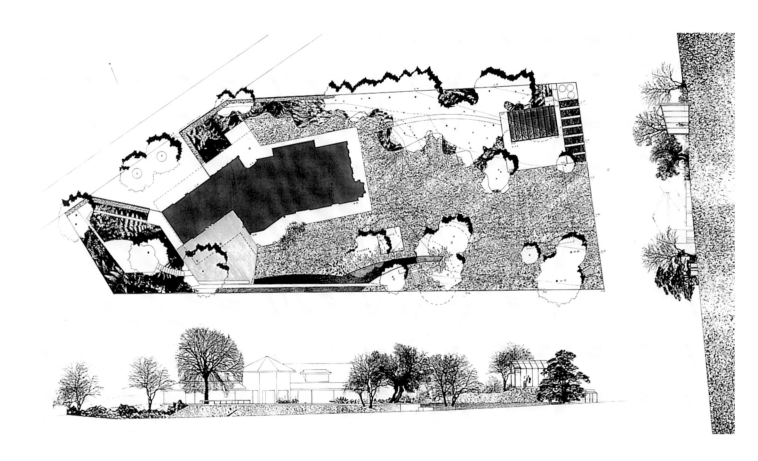

Garten Dr. B. in Herrliberg/Zürich
Projektplan Gartenumbau und Neubau
Orangerie 1995
Architekten Orangerie:
Ch. Gautschi + B. Storrer, Zürich
Grundriß, Schnitte
Original 1:100, 65 x 120 cm; Tusche,
Folie auf Großxerox, weiß

Garden Dr. B. in Herrliberg/Zurich
Project plan for garden conversion
and new construction orangery 1995
Architects orangery:
Ch. Gautschi + B. Storrer, Zurich
Ground plan, sections
Original 1:100, 65 x 120 cm; ink, foil on
white Xerox copy

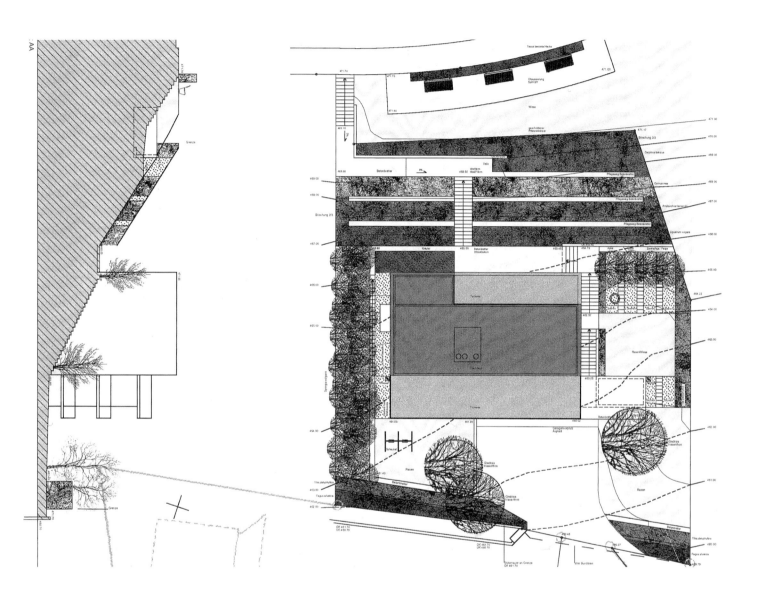

Garten Prof. J. in Küsnacht/Zürich
Architekten U. Marbach + A. Rüegg, Zürich
Projektplan Gartenneubau 1996
CAD Grundriß, Schnitt
Original 1:100, 29 x 43 cm

Garden Prof. J. in Kusnacht/Zurich
Architects U. Marbach + A. Rüegg, Zurich
Project plan new garden construction 1996
CAD ground plan, section
Original 1:100, 29 x 43 cm

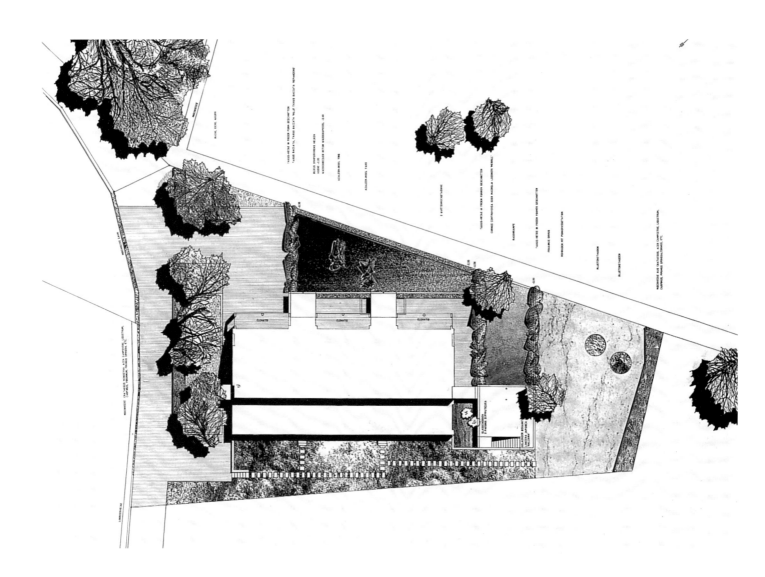

Garten F.-K. in Meggen/Luzern
Projektplan Gartenneubau 1996
Grundriß
Original 1:100, 50 x 70 cm; Tusche, Folie und
Kreide auf grauem Großxerox

Garden F.-K. in Meggen/Luzern
Project plan new garden construction 1996
Ground plan
Original 1:100, 50 x 70 cm; ink, foil
and crayon on gray Xerox copy

Weitere Gartenprojekte

Additional Garden Projects

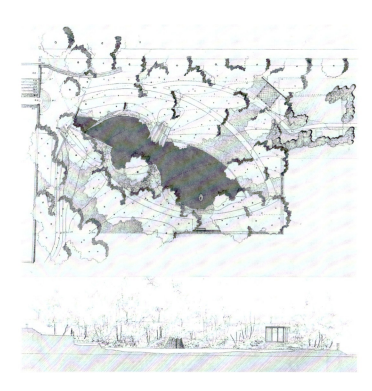

Garten W. in Küsnacht/Zürich
Projektplan Gartenumänderung mit Pool 1989
Grundriß, Schnitte, Axonometrie
Original 1:100, 60 x 120 cm; Bleistift auf grauem
Halbkarton
nicht realisiert

Garden W. in Kusnacht/Zurich
Project plan garden conversion with pool 1989
Ground plan, sections, axonometry
Original 1:100, 60 x 120 cm; pencil on gray
semi-cardboard
unrealized

Schloß G. im Kanton Bern
Projektplan mit neuen Gartenteil 1991
Grundriß, Schnitte
Original 1:100, 68 x 113 cm; Bleistift und
Kreide auf Transparent
nicht realisiert

Castle G. in the Canton of Bern
Project plan with new garden section 1991
Ground plan, sections
Original 1:100, 68 x 113 cm; pencil and crayon
on transparency
unrealized

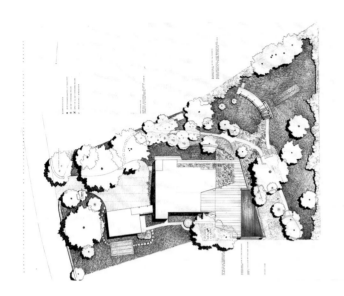

Garten Sch. in Küsnacht/Zürich
Projektplan Gartenumänderung 1992
Grundriß
Original 1:100, 66 x 90 cm; Bleistift und
Ölkreide auf grauem Halbkarton
nicht realisiert

Garden Sch. in Kusnacht/Zurich
Project plan garden conversion 1992
Ground plan
Original 1:100, 66 x 90 cm; pencil and
oil crayon on gray semi-cardboard
unrealized

Garten K. in Ittigen/Bern
Architekten H. Gafner + B. Kaufmann, Zürich und Ittigen
Projektplan Garten zu Wohn- und Geschäftshaus 1993
Grundriß
Original 1:100, 70 x 100 cm; Bleistift und Farbstift
auf grauem Halbkarton
teilweise realisiert

Garden K. in Ittigen/Bern
Architects H. Gafner + B. Kaufmann, Zurich and Ittigen
Project plan garden for an apartment/office building 1993
Ground plan
Original 1:100, 70 x 100 cm; pencil and
colored pencil on gray semi-cardboard
partially realized

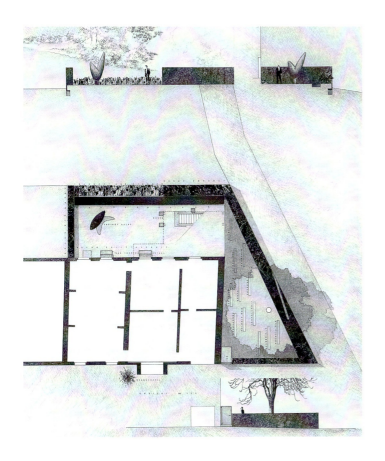
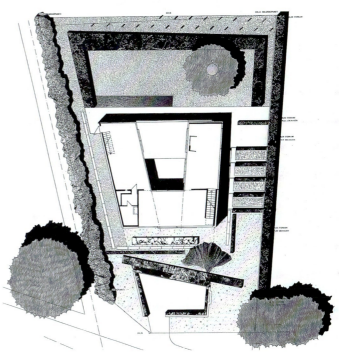

Garten F. in Schaffhausen
Projektplan Garten zu historischem Wohnhaus 1993
Grundriß, Schnitte
Original 1:50, 70 x 100 cm; Tusche, Folie und Farbstift
auf grauem Halbkarton
nicht realisiert

Garden F. in Schaffhausen
Project plan garden for a historic apartment house 1993
Ground plan, sections
Original 1:50, 70 x 100 cm; ink, foil and colored pencil
on gray semi-cardboard
unrealized

Garten K. in Riehen /Basel
Architekten Herzog & de Meuron, Basel
Projektplan Gartenneubau 1994
Grundriß
Original 1:100, 45 x 60 cm Tusche; Folie, Farbstift
auf grauem Großxerox
nicht realisiert

Garden K. in Riehen/Basel
Architects Herzog & de Meuron, Basel
Project plan new garden construction 1994
Ground plan
Original 1:100, 45 x 60 cm; ink, foil, colored pencil
on gray Xerox copy
unrealized

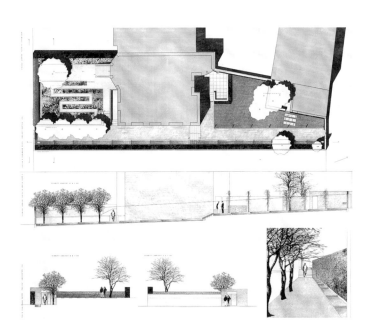
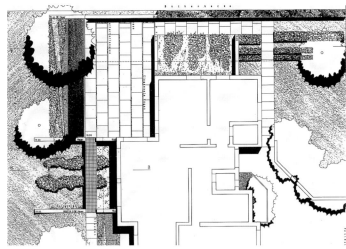

Garten F. In Basel
Projektplan Gartenumbau 1994
Grundriß, Schnitte, Perspektive
Original 1:50, 49 x 118 cm; Tusche, Folie,
Farbstift auf weißem Plandruck
nicht realisiert

Garden F. in Basel
Project plan garden conversion 1994
Ground plan, sections, perspective
Original 1:50, 49 x 118 cm; ink, foil,
colored pencil on white planprint
unrealized

Garten C. in Adliswil/Zürich
Projektplan Gartenumänderung 1995
Grundriß
Original 1:50, 60 x 80 cm; Tusche,
Folie auf weißem Großxerox
realisiert

Garden C. in Adliswil/Zurich
Project plan garden conversion 1995
Ground plan
Original 1:50, 60 x 80 cm; ink, foil
on white Xerox copy
realized

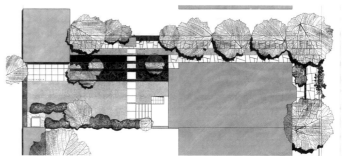

Garten M. in Ronco/Tessin
Projektplan Gartenneubau 1995
Grundriß, Schnitt, Perspektive
Original 1:50 , 60 x 84 cm; Tusche,
Folie auf weißem Großxerox
nicht realisiert

Garden M. in Ronco/Ticino
Project plan garden conversion 1995
Ground plan, section, perspective,
Original 1:50, 60 x 84 cm; ink, foil
on white Xerox copy
unrealized

Garten Dr. F. in Basel
Projektplan Gartenumänderung
zu Wohnhaus 1995
CAD Grundriß
Original 1:50, 40 x 95 cm
teilweise realisiert

Garden Dr. F. in Basel
Project plan garden conversion
for an apartment house 1995
CAD ground plan
Original 1:50, 40 x 95 cm
partially realized

Alle vorgestellten Gärten wurde in unserem Zürcher Büro geplant. Bis 1994 unter dem Namen Stöckli, Kienast & Koeppel, Landschaftsarchitekten, Zürich und Bern. Seit 1995 heißt unser Büro «Kienast Vogt Partner Landschaftsarchitekten Zürich und Bern». Deren Inhaber sind Erika Kienast-Lüder, Günther Vogt und Dieter Kienast. An der Planung und Realisierung der vorgestellten Gärten waren folgende Mitarbeiterinnen und Mitarbeiter beteiligt: David Bosshard, Peter Hüsler, Fabienne Kienast, André Müller, Nicole Newmark, Thomas Steinmann, Andres Tremp, Erich Zwahlen.

Die Photos wurden von Christian Vogt, Basel in den Jahren 1991–96 aufgenommen. Als einzige Ausnahme stammen die Photos von Chaumont-sur-Loire von Wolfram Müller, Karlsruhe.

Bis auf zwei Objekte, den Garten Villa Wehrli und den Ausstellungsgarten in Chaumont-sur-Loire, handelt es sich um private Gärten. Ihre Besitzer möchten auch weiterhin ihr privates «Gartenreich» erleben. Deshalb bitten wir die geschätzten Leserinnen und Leser, von unangemeldeten Besuchen abzusehen. Für allfällige Besuchswünsche wenden Sie sich bitte an unser Büro.

All gardens presented above were planned in our Zurich office. Until 1994 under the name Stoeckli, Kienast & Koeppel, landscape architects, Zurich and Bern. Since 1995 our office is called "Kienast Vogt Partner landscape architects, Zurich and Bern". The proprietors are Erika Kienast-Lüder, Günther Vogt and Dieter Kienast. The following collaborators assisted us in the planning and realization of the introduced garden designs: David Bosshard, Peter Hüsler, Fabienne Kienast, André Müller, Nicole Newmark, Thomas Steinmann, Andres Tremp, Erich Zwahlen.

The pictures were taken by Christian Vogt, Basel, from 1991–96. The only exceptions are the pictures of Chaumont-sur-Loire, which were taken by Wolfram Müller, Karlsruhe.

Except for two objects, the garden for the Wehrli Villa and the exhibition garden in Chaumont-sur-Loire, all of the gardens are on private property. Their owners wish to continue to enjoy their private "garden kingdom". We therefore kindly ask our esteemed readers to refrain from any unannounced visits. If you wish to visit a garden, please contact our office. Thank you.